CW00657309

To my sons, Harry and James. This book is for you.
I hope one day you will have work lives that you love.

CONTENTS

FOREWORD BY
LARRY OAKNER

For over three decades of employment, I have loved my work. Fundamentally a writer, I applied my way with words to earn a living in advertising, then branding, and finally, employee brand engagement. Of course, there were plenty of times when I truly disliked where I worked or who I worked with, but I always liked the creative process of bringing an idea to life as an ad, a brand positioning statement, or an employee engagement training program.

What is employee engagement? The way I define it is how employees understand, embrace, and express their corporate culture through their everyday behavior at work. As more companies have begun to embrace the idea of bringing their brands to life through their employees' day-to-day behaviors, I used my training as a college educator and creativity as a branding expert to develop award-winning workshop-based programs for major corporations, including

Caterpillar, Microsoft, Lilly, Girl Scouts of USA, ING, and Medtronic, to name a few of the hundreds I have worked with.

As my employee engagement practice grew at the branding firm where I spent my last dozen years, I needed to find a person who could help me enrich the offering, with more knowledge of how employees *feel* about their work. After interviewing a few candidates who weren't right, I met Rebecca Longman.

With her impeccable credentials in HR, her multiple degrees in Psychology, and global client experience, I knew I had found the right person. What Rebecca didn't know about corporate branding, I could teach her. What I didn't know about the psychology of work, she could school me. While I had always focused on training employees on their company's brand culture, Rebecca had been developing a way to help individual employees find their own path into corporate culture and ultimately love to work. The balance made us a great team.

At the first workshop we did together, for an Educational Publisher, Rebecca jumped into the pool fearlessly to lead a section of the training. I admired her courage but quickly came to her rescue as she wasn't quite ready to take on the branding part. Over time, we evolved a true partnership in which I learned from her as much as she learned from me. We collaborated on blog posts, podcasts, workshops, and dozens of corporate brand training sessions. We both focused on how employees can make the best of their jobs for themselves and for their company, which is an equally winning relationship for the company and the individual.

Let's Love to Work is the result of Rebecca's ability to connect an employee's emotional and professional perspectives at work. She has used her professional education and corporate training to develop a system to help individuals learn to love their work, rather than conform to a prescribed corporate behavior. In her book, Rebecca shares how Career Agents, as she calls them, have developed work lives that they love. Through her interviews with workers from around the world, she has identified how people can create fulfilling work lives without sacrificing their souls. She brings a sense of humanity to the workplace that enables people to embrace their careers—embrace as in love.

About Larry Oakner

Starting his career as an award-winning copywriter and advertising creative director on the West Coast, Larry moved to New York and became a brand strategist and the pioneering leader in internal branding and employee engagement, helping employees of Fortune 500 companies live their brand through conscious choices every day. Along his career, Oakner practiced his craft at prestigious branding firms such as Siegel & Gale, Interbrand and Tenet Partners where he created programs for clients such as Lockheed-Martin, Caterpillar, GE, Bayer, Medtronic, Microsoft, Conduent, and 3M to name a few of the hundreds of clients he has helped.

Larry has written extensively in the media about employee engagement and branding. He has taught advertising marketing communications as an adjunct professor SUNY-Fashion Institute of Technology in Manhattan. He holds a Bachelor of Arts and a Master's Degree in Teaching English, Cum Laude, from UCLA. Oakner is also the author of the industry book, *And Now A Few Laughs From Our Sponsor: The Best Fifty Years of Radio Commercials* (Wiley/Adweek, 2002).

PREFACE

The world of work is changing. The global pandemic has caused many of us to reassess our lives in numerous ways, and how we work, where we work, and what we do for work are some of our foremost considerations. We are thinking not only about the work we do and what we enjoy or don't enjoy, but also about the *way* we work.

For many, the pandemic offered a welcome break from office life, while others found the lack of separation between work and home activities unsettling. Others, particularly those with young families, struggled to figure out how to work and care for children simultaneously. For those working in medical, retail, or hospitality settings, for example, the changes to safety protocols and the scary realities of going to work every day have made many reassess their career choices.

Of course, we all quickly realized that escaping work through lockdowns wasn't the solution to the work problems we faced, but the upheaval showed us the possibilities of working differently. One of the fallouts from the pandemic is record numbers of people changing jobs; many aren't comfortable with the way they once worked. The distance from the daily grind has given many the chance to realize problems with their job or discover what they truly dislike about their work.

Even before the pandemic hit, people were starting to question the way we were working. Commutes were often long or unnecessary, and the impact of travelling to and from work every day was damaging our environment. Many companies who said remote working wasn't possible were suddenly plunged into a scenario in which 'not possible' wasn't an option.

Whatever your experience, positive or negative, the pandemic has caused many of us to rethink our lives. While some of us will go back to the status quo, many others have made the decision to make drastic changes.

Unfortunately, making changes that could potentially turn our lives inside out isn't easy, and to find what truly works for us takes time, self-reflection, and support.

I've worked for over 13 years in the field of engaging people at work. I've had the pleasure of coaching and supporting people to rethink how they work. I've built systems and programs for global blue-chip companies to help improve employee engagement and motivation in the work-place. Most recently, I embarked on a research project to find out what makes people love their jobs and careers. This book is the result of that labor of love.

The combination of my knowledge, experience, and research has led me to finding one major aspect that surfaces time and time again by people who enjoy their work; they are all agents of their own careers. Every one of these people is different, with different agendas, backgrounds, educational attainment, and passions, but they all share the one common trait of making consistent, intentional decisions about how to shape their career into one that works for them.

Career Agents have created a sense of control over their working lives. That type of control looks different for everyone, but it's there in all cases. It is found in people who have shaped their working lives into something fulfilling, either off their own back or with support, encouragement, and drive from others. Career Agents don't necessarily love every minute of their jobs—although some do—but they love the majority of their work and have found ways, or are planning ways, to rid themselves of the work that doesn't excite them.

Through support from their carefully nurtured networks, they have found ways to map out working lives that fit around their out-of-work needs and that pay them the income they want and need to feel satisfied while doing the work they love most. They have found the people that cheerlead them on their paths to success; they have found ways to make their jobs work for them. They are not slaves to their working lives; they thrive on them.

In many ways, they are people who have dispelled with the cultural norms of how they or others think they should work, and they have charted their own paths. Some have built businesses, while others have made slight tweaks to the parameters of 'normal' working lives to meet their individual needs.

Career Agents recognize that, as much as the organizations they work for have a responsibility of making working lives safe, inspiring, and fulfilling, they can only go so far. Making your career into one that fulfils your needs is up to you.

In this book, I'm going to share with you *how* Career Agents, as I have dubbed them, have created the working lives they love, and I will provide tips for how *you* can do the same. These tips are informed by 17 in-depth interviews discussing what makes a person love to work, as well as many more conversations, and a lot of research.

My goal is that this book will help to guide you to a better understanding of what drives others at work and will show you the resources you can use to create a more engaged working life that works for you.

The following quote is from one of my interviewees. Meeting many people throughout my career who feel this way is one of the main reasons why I've written this book.

"I was putting so much work in, but I wasn't happy. I knew I was good at it, and I felt like I had trained myself up to be good at what I was doing, but I wasn't

feeling fulfilled. At that time, I had convinced myself that the problem was the company surroundings that I was working in, and if I changed company, everything would be ok. So, I did. In the new job, I didn't mind the hard work, but I then thought, 'What am I doing?' just came flooding back. Because I was struggling every day, I just didn't feel like myself. It's so easy to keep convincing yourself to stay, thinking 'this is what you've done for 13 years, the money is good, just enjoy yourself outside of work'. But that isn't possible, because you're grumpy all the time and exhausted. It impacts your relationships, and you know deep down that you're just wasting time." Bhavisha.

PART 1

WHY DO SO MANY PEOPLE DISLIKE WORK?

CHAPTER 1
WHY MOST PEOPLE
DISLIKE WORK

When I started my training in the concept of applying psychology at work, my tutor asked me why I wanted to work in the field. My response was "to help people". My education began there.

You see, when you're an organizational psychologist, often, the people you want to help aren't the people who pay your wages. The people who decide what programs you'll run or initiatives you'll design are the senior leaders in the company, and often, their agendas aren't focused on creating happy employees who love what they do. That will sound controversial to many, but that's not my intention. As much as there are leaders out there who want to create workplaces where their employees feel satisfied, driven, supported, and nurtured, any leader's primary goal in *any* organization, whether they want it to be or not, is to make the company profitable. Ultimately, companies exist to serve consumers' needs, and everything else becomes secondary.

For any company to survive, they must be profitable, and profit comes from an efficient, useful company that hires efficient, useful people who get the job done. If some leaders in these companies can help people have fulfilling careers along the way, that's a bonus, but it's not, and never will be, the primary goal. When you look at the big picture and remind yourself that an organization's primary goal is to make money, not look after their people, you begin to see that organizations' approach to motivating and engaging their employees is fundamentally flawed.

Often, systems and processes, such as training and development programs, reward and recognition approaches, and promotion ladders, don't have the impact that the managers and leaders of companies hoped for, and if they do, those impacts are short-lived. The reasons why they don't work or don't have a long-lasting impact are as follows:

a) The same rewards have less impact each time we receive them. When our motivation to work comes from external rewards (rather than intrinsic motivation or the desire to do a task because we enjoy the activity itself), we gradually want more or different rewards for the same work.

b) We're often required to learn skills that we don't want to learn or aren't good at and don't have the time to master. Furthermore, we, or the organizations we work for, generally aren't good at recognizing or making use of our natural talents or the work we most enjoy.

c) We don't feel trusted to deliver our work on our own terms.

The result? An employee ends up the opposite of what the organization was trying to achieve: demotivated, unheard, stressed, and ready to leave and start the process all over again at a new company.

Unfortunately, unless you happen to be in a senior position or a high performer, investment in you is rarely personalized. Organizations take a 'blanket' approach to motivating people at work because it's time-consuming, complex, and expensive to meet everyone's individual needs.

But happy employees are more productive employees.

While much research has been done into what makes employees do their best work, the programs designed to bring this research to life often don't get to the core of truly motivating people. Even though these programs can be designed with the best research in mind, the design is always done with background whispers: 'But how much is this going to cost?', 'How long will it take?', 'But we need results now!', and so on. Every HR team or consulting firm hired to 'fix' employee motivation has restraints to work within, so the outcome can never be fully employee-centric.

On top of this, leaders of companies, like any employees, have their own agendas, and there's no harm in that; we all have our own agendas. However, despite research suggesting that engaged and motivated employees help to make businesses more successful, efficient, and profitable, the pressures for leaders to meet deadlines and make their mark in short timeframes become the primary goals.

Employee engagement and motivation programs aren't a quick fix. They take time to design and implement and are expensive, and for leaders who want to make a big impact quickly, the results may not be fast enough.

While there are leaders who recognize that getting a company to operate at its best means doing everything they can to motivate and engage their employees, the nuances and realities of employee motivation are far more complicated than good pay, benefits, and giving people opportunities to learn and develop, however in-depth those solutions are designed to be.

Helping employees to be happy at work requires more than organizational programs.

Employee needs and motivations change often, sometimes daily. Their fundamental needs may stay the same, for example, to provide for their family or get a promotion, but motivation and engagement at work is a finely tuned balance that is impacted by so much more than simple fixes. Daily interactions with colleagues, external market pressures, workspaces, lives outside of work, the weather, and so much more influence how people work every day. Keeping employees motivated and happy at work is a massive feat and takes time, effort, commitment, and a deep understanding of workplace psychology.

As much as organizational psychology or HR practitioners may dislike admitting it, many of the programs they've helped build won't have the impacts they claim or hope they will have, simply because one approach can't meet everyone's needs. Unfortunately, many of these systems and processes will be as much use as a chocolate fire guard; they are never going to remain intact for long, and they will likely create a sticky mess when they fall apart. The more complicated you build them, the slower they may melt, but ultimately, they will never be a perfect fit for the job.

Some companies try extremely hard to motivate people, and that's commendable. But even when these initiatives work well, they are only part of the employee engagement puzzle. Meeting the needs of individual employees requires more than just an organization's employee motivation and engagement agenda.

Ultimately, what companies want and what you want, as employees, aren't the same. Your personal career fulfilment will never be your organization's most important goal. Nor should it be.

CHAPTER 2
HOW MORE PEOPLE
COULD ENJOY WORK

In the past, people have landed jobs and expected to remain in them for most of their working lives. Even up until the last 10–15 years, many people have expected to get a job and stick with it for a reasonable amount of time. But now, the landscape has changed; many individuals work in jobs for only a few years before they move to a new role. The result is people having careers made up of several pivots into different roles, companies, and ways of working.

Nowadays, you have to connect the dots between the different roles you decide to take and how you can transfer your skills from one position to the next while also giving something useful to the job you're doing at that point in time. You must continually decide if the next job you take will help further your career in the direction you want to take it. At the same time, you must determine if what you will be doing day-to-day not only gives you the skills, experience, or knowledge you want to gain, but if the culture of your job fits in with what matters to you and if you enjoy being there. We're no longer a society that accepts that work is just a way to pay the bills; we're recognizing more and more that the value of work is something that can enrich our lives.

Before we delve further into how to create a career you love, let's first look at what we mean by the word 'career'. 'Career' is a word with loaded connotations. When I used to think of the word 'career', I would imagine a person on Wall Street in NYC or standing outside Bank tube station in Central London, suited and booted and heading to the office to crunch numbers. Now I think of the word differently. I recognize that having a career isn't only for people in the corporate world. Careers are about shaping a working life out of the skills and desires you have or want to learn to allow you to enjoy your work and get paid fairly for it, whichever industry you work in.

Careers look vastly different for everyone; your options are almost endless. Unfortunately, the array of choices also means that it can be easy to find yourself on the wrong path.

When you feel stuck.

How many times have you gone into a new workplace full of hopes and dreams that this will be the place to make everything better? That this will be the workplace you've been dreaming of? That they will look after you, develop your skills, support you, and make your time there fulfilling, only to find, a few years down the line, that it's just like every other workplace.

You're bored, demotivated, disengaged, and looking for the nearest exit.

Unfortunately, these cycles don't change. People often come into the workplace expecting to find their dream job but end up disappointed because it's not what they thought it would be. Many feel they've taken the wrong career path and feel stuck. Some still think they're on the right path, but the reality of the job and what they thought it would be don't match.

However, when you remind yourself that an organization's primary goal is to serve their customers, not their employees, it makes sense for you to feel unsatisfied by your job role.

Sometimes, you can get to a point where your perspective of the environment in which you work has become toxic enough that you can't see what you need, or how to get what you need, to feel happier at work.

It's okay not to know what is making you feel unhappy or where you want to go next. The trick is being comfortable with the transition stage and knowing that, if you do the work, the clarity will come. It takes time to make changes in life, so we need to be patient with ourselves. We must give ourselves time to make well-thought-through decisions about where we want to go in life and how we want to get there. Knee-jerk decisions rarely result in positive outcomes. My grandmother's favorite saying was, 'Act in haste, repent at leisure'.

Your lack of motivation and engagement is a problem for the company you work for, but, more importantly, it's detrimental to you, too. The demotivation that you might experience at work results in more sick days and causes you to want to come into work late and leave early, even if you don't have somewhere you need to be, which affects your mental health both inside and outside of work. It can cause you to underperform in your tasks and not work productively or cooperatively with other team members or managers. It may also result in your neglect for others in the company instead of going over and above what's expected of you in your role. Demotivation can even eventually lead to a wish to leave the organization or getting fired after only a short time.

Dream jobs are two-way streets.

When we start working somewhere, we often put our fulfillment in the hands of the employer. We follow the paths laid out for us by them, we expect them to onboard us into the company, and we wait for them to teach us what we need to know to succeed. We take little responsibility for our experience in the role. Why should we, right? They hired us, and it's up to them to tell us what to do, how to do it, and when to do it.

Maybe that's not the best approach. Work is a relationship, and relationships are two-way streets. Having a healthy connection requires effort and compromise from both parties. Just like my interviewee, Denny, explains:

"You have to be intentional about [your work]. It's like a great relationship; when you're in love with someone, you're intentional about it." Denny.

All the facilitation in the world can come from the managers and leaders around you, but if you hate your work or co-workers, or don't feel something pulling you to stay where you are, their efforts will fall flat. As an employee, you need to feel a connection to your work to feel motivated and engaged, and you can only feel such a connection when you understand your own working needs and what drives you at work. Passively going along with work because it's your manager's or leader's role to make it so, or because you have resigned yourself to the fact that you can find fulfillment outside of work is not a good way to live life.

If you went along passively in other parts of your life, how would it feel? Would you let someone else choose everything you eat, drink, or wear? Or would you prefer to make those conscious decisions yourself because they are part of what make you a person?

Why do so many of us allow someone else to make the decisions for how we work?

We often accept jobs without really thinking about what we need from them. As long as we get a paycheck and some kind of general satisfaction', we think we will be ok. But when you go to work each day and don't think consciously about whether it's working for you or what you could do to make it better, you are effectively relinquishing the control of your happiness, engagement, development, and productivity. You're letting someone else map your career and happiness at work.

The need to take control of your working life is particularly important when considering that there is no real loyalty between organizations and their employees. As one of my interviewees reminded me, when employees are no longer needed, they are out the door within two weeks, sometimes the same day.

The power of taking control.

Leaders of companies have a responsibility to make the workplace fulfilling for you, with opportunities to grow, learn, and develop, but your happiness is not a one-way street.

Throughout my career, I've realized that those who have remained engaged in their work, and continued to outperform those who aren't so engaged, took responsibility for their own careers. *They* decided if the systems and approaches that the company put in place were right for them, and if they weren't, they found ways to influence their situation to meet their needs. It was down to them to enjoy what they do, and they actively shaped their careers to ensure their own happiness.

Being a Career Agent might seem like a tall order. How do you change from assuming that your company is responsible for how your working life plays out to realizing that it is up to you?

Firstly, let's briefly think about the benefits of being your own Career Agent:

- Lower stress levels due to feeling happier both inside and outside of work.

- Working more efficiently to get better results, which often results in higher income and a better chance of promotion.

- Feeling more energized and willing to go the extra mile for your company. In turn, your leaders, managers, and peers will want to do the same for you.

- Work will be something you *want* to do rather than something you *must* do.

When you understand what drives you and why and find ways to bring more of those things into your job, work can become a source of happiness, excitement, and accomplishment. Work can be a positive addition to your life rather than something you must do to feed your life outside it.

However, individuals who love their work don't always love *everything* they do. Career Agents have an overarching vision of their own career path and where they want their lives to go outside their current job role. They have a bigger picture view that spurs them on, even when some parts of their day aren't fulfilling them.

People who love to work take ownership of their careers in ways that most aren't even aware of. They know themselves and what makes them tick; they are their own Career Agents.

It's not *all* down to you, but most of it is.

It is still the responsibility of employers to provide us with fulfilling workplaces.

Business owners have accountability to help motivate their workers, support their growth, and provide them with safe, respectful environments. However, our motivation at work, in many ways, is up to us. We have access to many resources to help take our careers wherever we want them to go, and we can shape that growth in any way we choose.

As the saying goes, we come into this world alone and we go out of it alone. To love what we do, we must take responsibility for our own engagement in our working lives; we must become our own Career Agents.

The following quote highlights how important it is to make decisions that work for you:

"I thought I could work for the same company for life; I could be traveling and working around the globe. And then the recession happened ... and effectively, the organization retrenched and made a lot of people redundant. I started to realize you can't really trust a large organization to have your needs at their heart, and you need to think about what you want, what drives you, and that was when I started thinking about making my own path." Maurice.

Maurice went on to tell me about someone he knows who stayed at a company for 30 years and loved it. You must do what's right for you. Take control of your own path, whatever that path may be. Taking ownership of your path may mean changing some things in your life, which can be difficult. It's much easier to give that responsibility to someone else and blame them if it doesn't work out. But that will only leave you miserable at work and at a loss for how to create a career you love. I'm here to show you how to take ownership of your career and how you can become your own Career Agent.

This book will show you what others have done to create careers they love and the psychological traits and behaviors that helped them do it.

PART 2

WHAT MAKES PEOPLE LOVE TO WORK?

CHAPTER 3
WHAT PEOPLE WHO LOVE TO WORK ACTUALLY DO

Do you often find yourself asking the following questions?

- How can I be happier at work?

- How can I create a career and life for myself that makes me enjoy work while staying in my current job?

- How can I change my career into something I like but still retain my income?

There are lots of blog posts and articles that suggest doing this or that to create a happier work experience, but *how* do you go about finding what truly motivates you?

Motivation and engagement are truly an individual experience, and what works for you might not work for someone else. That's why it's important to look past *what* engages and motivates us and others and to think about *how* we can find what drives us.

- What steps do I need to take to truly make my work life happier?

- Is it a good idea to mix what I love outside of work with what I do in work? Or should I just 'get on with work' and live for life outside it?

- Does money matter to me? If so, how much matters?

Building a career you love from the ground up.

To support you to love your work, I felt I needed to teach you how to recognize and learn to use the tools you already have. I'm not here to help you find a particular job or improve your resumé; I'm here to share with you what I've learnt from other people who love their work and show how you can apply those learnings to your own work life.

My goal is to assist you with your personal engagement from the ground up, with a clearer picture of what *you* want to do so that you can take your engaged self on any career path you choose.

You will find work that inspires you, and whichever organization you choose to work for will have an employee who better understands themselves and how to take their career in the direction that best suits their skills, qualifications, mindset, and needs.

I'm going to help you answer the following questions:

- Which psychological tools can I successfully apply to my working life?

- How can I navigate the world of work to create a career and life for myself that makes me happy regardless of how my current workplace operates?

- Which steps do I need to take to truly make my life at work happier?

- How do I put my own self-development first when the company I'm in wants me to train in areas I don't care about to meet the needs of their business?

- How do I find what truly motivates me?

Should you love work?

I often hear the phrase 'do what you love' being discussed amongst my peers. I see it written frequently in blogs and articles about creating a life you love and finding work that doesn't drain you. I see people handing out such advice when their friends, co-workers, or family members complain about the monotony of their jobs, or the lack of career progression or creativity allowed in their roles. I've also seen and heard it be said to people who are stuck in careers they dislike because of the income they need.

'Do what you love' seems like a fix-all for work woes. But is it? My response is always 'not exactly'. I believe there is some weight to following this philosophy, but, as a standalone idea, it's far too simple to be useful.

The phrase 'do what you love' suggests that people should or must *find* work they love to feel fulfillment in their career. My research has shown me that these thought processes make people believe either that if they can't *find* that *one thing* they love to do, then they have failed in their career or, if they are not loving every part of what they do every single day, then they are in the wrong job. I wholeheartedly believe neither of these ideas to be true.

No-one 'hates work'.

When I was studying for my master's degree in Occupational Psychology in 2010, one of my professors said to me that, too often he hears the phrase 'people dislike change'.

What he said next surprised me: the statement 'people dislike change' is wholly untrue. I looked at him inquisitively, expecting him to tell me that, secretly, people love change and that only trained psychologists can understand how to read the plethora of struggles caused by change as positive experiences. What else could he mean?

He explained that no one dislikes 'change' per-se; it is certain factors associated with the change that people dislike. The key to understanding people's emotions about a changing situation, and how to react to those emotions, is to understand the essence of what the person dislikes about *that specific change of scenario*. The same goes for a job or career.

If someone is complaining that they hate their job, it's important to peel away the layers of discontent to understand which specific parts the person hates and why they hate them. Do they truly dislike those parts of their work? Perhaps certain factors have beaten them down enough in their career to have *caused* them to dislike the parts of their work that they used to like.

It is possible that someone *could* dislike everything they do, but there may be more to the story. This is why peeling back those layers to get to the core of the issue is an important first step towards finding what truly motivates you at work. In the process, you may even find some parts of your work that you didn't realize you enjoy and look for ways to increase those other positive parts of your job.

The key to knowing what makes work enjoyable or not is knowing what you value. If you know what matters to you and you can design your life in a way that meets those needs (even if it's not all of them), you will feel more fulfilled and be closer to loving your work.

What you love is complicated.

The idea that one can love *all* of what they do every day is unrealistic. Just like in any area of life, there are always good and bad bits, and we learn to take the rough with the smooth.

No relationship is positive all of the time. People in all kinds of relationships frequently say and do things that cause upset, but this doesn't make us immediately give up on those relationships. We weather the rough times because the good outweighs the bad. We only begin to be concerned when the bad times overshadow the good.

With this in mind, it is clear that you don't *need* to do what you *love* day in day out to find joy in your work. The key is finding a balance between the things you like and don't like and making sure there are more of the former than the latter. Unfortunately, many of you are yet to discover what you love to do or how to incorporate it into your work.

Fulfilment can be found in the most unlikely places.

A couple of summers ago, I joined a local running club. One evening, a rep from the local sneaker shop joined us for our weekly run. The rep, Chris, shared with me how he loves to hike and run and that he wanted a job that allowed him to do those things on a more regular basis:

> *"I couldn't imagine sitting behind a desk every day, and I never thought a job in sales would be the answer."* Chris.

He went on to tell me that he had spent much of his childhood exploring the outdoors, so had connections with sporting facilities and stores. He spoke to one of his contacts one day about the potential of starting a role at a store and they told him about the opportunity to travel the tri-state area selling their sneakers. They told him he would have a lot of control over his time and work, but he would have targets to meet. He knew the job would involve lots of driving and encouraging people to buy the sneakers, but he'd used the sneakers himself and he believed in the quality of the brand. He said, "it's an easy sell for me". He also knew that the best way to sell running sneakers to people is to catch them in the environment they most use them—out running. He realized he'd be able to earn a living while being surrounded by sport, which outweighed the downside of large amounts of driving, making it the perfect role for him.

Chris told me that he never thought he'd become a salesman, but that's not really what he sees himself as. He said he provides comfortable and suitable clothing, which he sees is vitally important for those interested in sport. He also has the opportunity to run outside and train with people with similar passions. For him, it's a win–win scenario.

Chris knows what drives him and how he can support other people to live the dream of exercising comfortably and effectively. He is highly engaged in what he does. He found a way to shape what he loves by using the outlet of something that he thought would never drive him: sales. Had Chris got a job in sales in a different field, he would never have been as engaged in his work. Sometimes it's not about the actual job that drives us, it's the factors that surround the job.

The factors that help you find work you love.

From conducting research interviews, working as a consultant helping to create tools, systems, and processes that help people find more motivation at work, and coaching numerous people to build careers they love, I have found that there are six major factors that help people build working lives they love:

1. Recognizing that value isn't the same as income.

2. Shaping one's own destiny and defining a broader personal purpose in their work.

3. Creating careers that meet the flexibility they require to allow them to meet the responsibilities they have outside of work.

4. Taking opportunities and risks to develop oneself and skills in ways that motivate and engage.

5. Receiving feedback from the people, tools, and influences that best suit them and filtering out what doesn't serve them.

6. Finding mentors or other inspirational sources to help guide them.

We will delve into each of these factors over the next six chapters.

CHAPTER 4
RECOGNIZING THAT VALUE
ISN'T THE SAME AS INCOME

To begin with, let's look at the biggest extrinsic motivator of all: money. As I listened to my interviewees share their stories about what money means to them when doing the work that they love, I could hear the resistance they felt to needing money to survive and how that need affects their work choices. They recognized that money is a vital part of life but that a fulfilling and happy life does not necessarily come from having money.

Many of my interviewees shared how they'd wrestled with the need for an income while charting their paths towards work that fulfils them. Some didn't even mention their struggles to reconcile doing what they truly wanted to do, the work they feel compelled to do, and their innate need to provide for their loved ones. But I could hear the subtle silences while they searched for the words to conceal their disappointment, having felt the need to curtail their desires in exchange for more income to support their families.

Money doesn't buy happiness.

At age 23 and in my first 'real job' in the Big City, I was earning a salary I'd believed was well out of my reach. I was excited. As my colleagues and I spilled out of work at the end of our day, the pubs would be full of people like us, drinking away the money we'd earned that day. One night, I had a few too many drinks and, before I knew it, I was telling anyone who would listen how proud I was of my new salary. It was then that a more senior colleague nudged me to shut my mouth and promptly changed the subject. His response made me recognize how naïve my actions were, since in many workplace settings, it is not acceptable to discuss what you earn.

However, I believe that not talking about what we earn puts financial income on a pedestal; it makes it seem like income is the holy grail of job satisfaction. We do need a reliable income to survive, and while higher salaries give us more opportunities to pay for things and experiences that we may not otherwise have access to, work can give us so much more than an income. Work itself can also be a source of life satisfaction.

Balance money and passion.

The desire to balance money and passion is a well-told story when it comes to careers. I talked about the balance at length with my interviewees. I've overheard colleagues and strangers discussing it in the cafeteria and in coffee shops, and I've had many discussions with my friends and family about what we should or could do that would make work and our passions both satisfying and financially stable. Unfortunately, it's also a balance that many people find difficult to find.

How much money do you need to give you the quality of life you want and require while also bringing you joy and fulfilment? What can you do that doesn't drain every ounce of pleasure you have in your life and have you dreading Monday morning?

It's never easy to create that balance. It can take time, patience, sacrifice, and a true understanding of what you require financially to be able to meet your needs.

One of my interviewees, Nadia, an Organizational Psychologist, often has to balance this struggle. She currently has two work agendas; one is her paid job working for her consulting firm, focusing on creating programs that support fathers who want to take parental leave and mothers who want to return to work. The other is a "non-profit company with the goal of creating psychologically safe environments that enable primary school children to be who they want to be, not what society thinks they should be."

"I need to have enough money to support and feed my family and make sure we have the lifestyle we want while not feeling like we're constantly watching the pennies. If I stopped [my consulting work] and just

focused on my nonprofit role, my family would seriously feel the impact. So, this is about a balance for me. " Nadia

I found Nadia's situation one of the most inventive approaches to doing what you love.

Nadia sees both of her endeavors as work, whether they bring her income or not, and she finds both fulfilling. The income is important to her, but she has calculated what she needs to feel satisfied and has found ways to make her passions influence her work, whether it's fee paying or not.

She has made two distinct decisions to allow her to meet her income and personal goals:

1. She started the non-profit role that she mentions above, allowing her to further her mission.

2. She continues her mission in work that she knows can command a salary, using her skillset as an organizational psychologist. She uses her skillset in a way that allows her to do work aligned to her mission.

What I find particularly interesting is how these two paths are distinct but link to one another to affect the same goal: creating a better balance between male and female roles in society.

Making the right work choices is key to loving what you do.

Nadia found a way to drive her mission forward while making the income she needs for her family and tackling her goal from the grass roots. By tackling the issue from two different perspectives, one that allows her to make an income and one that she uses her spare time to do, she not only gives her agenda more chance for success, but she also enables one endeavor to financially feed the other.

Another of my interviewee's balances paid and unpaid work to allow her the freedom to do her creative work. Emily runs a story-based writing service using techniques drawn from sales, public relations, and creative writing. She is also a creative writer and was chosen as one of the Penguin Random House Write Now Authors for 2018.

She told me her dual goals—getting the income she needs and writing short stories—and how getting regular client work will help her balance them:

> *"My goal with the content marketing was always to get just enough clients to keep the money ticking over. I have some clients that I work with on a retainer basis and others who give me a brief; I do it, and then it's done. With those kinds of jobs, I get enough in the bank to warrant spending more time doing creative work."* Emily.

Emily and Nadia offer two examples of how to find a financial and personal balance. Only you have the insight into what you need to earn, how to earn it, and what you're prepared to sacrifice to do what you enjoy, but learning how others find this balance can help you discover what might be possible.

Sometimes, finding that balance can be hard. There are times when you must put some of your aspirations and values aside to provide income. When this happens, finding ways to keep your passions alive within those compromises is key to loving what you do. It's not always an easy trade-off, but people who love what they do have found the balance between what they love and the income they need to make.

Bhavisha is an IT business partner and relationships manager, but she has also built a side business as a career coach. She uses many of her coaching skills in her full-time work, but she also found that, when her financial needs were covered, she had space to further explore her passion: helping people who feel stuck in jobs they hate:

"I have to go into work to earn, which is difficult because I feel like I am being a little bit hypocritical, but it takes the pressure off, allowing me to create something on the side that really serves people." Bhavisha.

She believes she will be able to leave her day job at some point and work solely on her own business. However, even if she doesn't reach that goal, or if it takes a long time, she has reshaped her full-time job role that she found draining in other settings into one that brings her some joy:

"I wanted to be in a culture that has high values, with people who respect one another, and I wasn't going to do just any job; I made sure I was going into a work-place where the people and culture were what I needed to survive." Bhavisha.

Virginia, a self-taught artist, made a very distinct choice to follow her financial goals rather than her passions from the beginning of her career:

"Even though I've always liked drawing and painting since I was a child, I didn't see this as a career path because, in Argentina, there is not much funding for the arts. My parents didn't have the means to support me through my studies, and I was the eldest amongst my siblings, so I needed to get a job right away after finishing high school. So, I became an early years teacher." Virginia.

Much of Virginia's early career focused on teaching, but she didn't let that stop her from living her passion:

"[Early years teaching] wasn't my first choice as a career, but I still enjoyed it because it had some [artistic] aspects that I used to motivate [the children]. I tried to

be the best teacher I could be, using the things I like to do, like drawing and painting, and it was really great for me and for some of the kids." Virginia.

Many of my interviewees channel what they enjoy into their work by being deliberate about what they want to do within their current roles and how they want to do it. They make choices that allow them to shape their current roles and, consequently, open up opportunities for future positions.

Another of my interviewees, Elizabeth, struck me with the intentionality that she displayed throughout her career to define her own path. She was always mindful about what she wanted to do and how she wanted to do it. If the defined path at her organization didn't meet those goals, she would find a way to make it work for her.

"I'm quite picky about the things I do, projects I get involved in at work, and the roles I go for." Elizabeth.

When she spoke about her work, it was with a sense of ownership over what she does and how she does it. She clearly understood that how her career played out was her responsibility and no-one else's. There were many times in Elizabeth's career when she felt she was doing something that she didn't enjoy, and each time, she made a considered effort to change her path. One of those times was when she was working as a people manager, and it wasn't playing to her strengths:

"[I didn't like] the people management side of the job in terms of managing people's feelings and positioning things in the right way all the time… [it] used to really frustrate me because I just wanted to move forward with [doing the tasks rather than educating or coaching others to do them]. When an opportunity came up for a secondment on the business process improvement team, I went for it and got it. I spent a year being an individual contributor. I loved that role; I loved not being on a team with people to manage because I knew my time was my own. Life was no longer about being a counselor, parent, and manager rolled into one; I could actually get on and get some results, and it was just so much better. I realized this was the path I wanted to take." Elizabeth.

Losing your way.

Unfortunately, there are times when you have to sacrifice passion for income, and it's all too easy to fall into the trap that so many people find themselves in: being stuck in a job you hate, much like Bhavisha's experience:

"I feel like I trained myself up to be good at what I was doing, but I knew I wasn't feeling fulfilled. At that time, I'd convinced myself that it was the surroundings and the company's fault and if I changed company, everything would be ok … so I did. [In the new job] I

did the hard work, but the same feelings came flooding back. I was struggling every day; I just didn't feel like myself." Bhavisha.

Bhavisha told me that she had started a career in IT because she'd wanted to be set up financially and ensure her family were proud of her career choices. At that time, she worried little about whether it was the right path for her, because her work allowed her to travel extensively, which she loved, and she had a very active social life. Her actual job role didn't matter too much to her then because it gave her the freedom to live an adventurous and gregarious life outside of work. However, as the years went on, she wanted to travel less and settle down, and she realized that the path she'd chosen wasn't fulfilling her. Unfortunately, at this point in her career, making changes meant she'd have to settle for a lesser income. Even though she knew what she was doing wasn't making her happy, she had no idea what else she wanted to do or could do with her skillset.

She embarked on an adventure, one she is still pursuing now four years later, to find her passion. She initially thought she could look at advertised jobs for inspiration to find out what other careers she should be doing.

She spent time shadowing a yoga instructor in California, learning how to make jewelry in London, baking bread at a café local to her home in London, and more.

Unfortunately, nothing worked, and she soon found she needed to look inward if she was going to find what she loves. She then spent many of the next few years receiving coaching, writing in journals, and exploring her inner desires to find what truly makes her tick.

Ultimately, she found that what inspires her is helping others who are in similar predicaments to hers, so she's now building her own coaching and training business.

However, the decision to start her own side business has not prevented Bhavisha from needing to work full time for income to support her family. The difference between her work now and roles she had in the past is that she is clearer about how she wants to operate in her day job. She knows that coaching and mentoring others is an important part of what she loves in her work, so she brings those skills into her role as an IT Business Partner. She enjoys her job much more than before even though the work she does is similar, but her perspective and approach to the work has changed.

Bhavisha's story perfectly illustrates the importance of exploring yourself and what matters to you to allow you to find work that you love.

Tune into your values.

At the beginning of my career, I had an altercation with a global head of HR. The HR director wanted a 100% response rate from the 60,000-person organization for their employee engagement survey, and she wanted me and a small team of HR minions to make it so.

The common assumption about survey response rates is that they need to be very high. It is not uncommon to hear people say that they require feedback from as many people as possible to gain a true reflection of the state of engagement in their workplace. In fact, to achieve a statistically valid figure, you only need a response from a representative sample of the population.

However, despite being a business psychologist trained in statistical analysis, it wasn't the statistics that sprung to my mind; it was my conviction that people should never be forced to do anything they don't want to do. Not only is this immoral, but it would skew the results since their hands had been forced.

I could have used a rational statistical argument to counter the HR Director's proposal, but I led with my heart. I took the moral high ground, arguing passionately about why people matter more than figures, and after months of back and forth, my lack of compliance got me fired.

Back then, I had few responsibilities aside from my own rent and food. I had no family to support, and I knew I could find another job to pay my way. I had the option to follow my morals without worrying about my financial goals. Would I make the same decision now as an expat wife and mother of two young children? Probably. I might handle it differently, but my morals and values haven't changed. I still strongly believe that people deserve to have a voice.

Should you do what I did? That's up to you. I've always led with my heart, but the choices you make are up to you and depend on how you want your career and life to play out.

Learning that I tend to lead with my heart meant that, when I was looking for my next role, I knew I should find something that allowed me to live my values more readily. Until I was put in that situation, I wasn't fully aware of how important these factors are to me. However, there are definitely easier ways to find your values than getting yourself fired!

Finding what you value.

What you value in life is an important part of finding work that you love. However, understanding what matters to you requires investing time in yourself to understand what makes you tick. That doesn't mean if you're doing something that doesn't align with your values you should quit immediately; it means that it's important to recognize that there could be more for you out there and you could start exploring what's possible.

Yasmin is a newly qualified psychotherapist. She knew from quite a young age that she wanted to become a therapist, but she needed to explore herself and her desires further first because she didn't feel fully confident in her decision to follow a path that mattered to her when it didn't please others. Sometimes, society, family, or peer pressure makes you feel there are certain career paths you should follow when your heart tells you to take a different path. She also recognized that, to follow the training path required to do what she wanted, she would first need a secure income.

"Trying to separate yourself from what [society expects you to do] is really important, but you need to feel stable enough to be able to think about what you want to do and consider your options. If you're panicking [about your income], you might end up doing something you don't want to do." Yasmin.

This book is not a detailed guide to help you find your values; there are many other resources out there that can help you do that.

But here are a few pointers to start your thinking:

1. Research a list of common values and choose a collection that resonate with you most.

2. Think of times, at work or at home, when you felt you lost track of time while you worked, or you came out of a task feeling exhilarated and excited to continue. Where were you and what were you doing?

3. Consider what makes you most frustrated, irritated, and angry at work or at home; what makes your blood boil?

When something creates such strong emotions in you, it's a sign that the underlying reason for that reaction is due to something you value.

4. Think of times when you offered to do something for another even though it didn't immediately bring you any benefits. What is driving you to do this? Perhaps the task you offered to help with is something that interests you, or perhaps you enjoy the feeling of supporting someone else. Think deeply about why you were driven to help; this is another key to understand your values.

The answers to these questions will give you clues as to the things in life that you value the most.

Activities

1. **Rate your values** in order of what you value most to what you value least. You may find some come out as equally important, and that's okay. The idea is to develop a list that helps you understand what is important to you. Only then can you begin to put the wheels in motion to make changes.

2. **Work out what you absolutely can't stomach.** What are the things that you really must change because they are causing you serious unhappiness?

Matthew, a product designer who works for a large kitchen manufacturer, gave me an example of something that he couldn't tolerate at work. Matthew's company took him on a trip to Indonesia to visit one of the factories where kitchens are made. When he was there, he saw a young man who he guessed was around 13 or 14 making cupboard doors. He noted that it wasn't one of the factories his company used as a supplier but seeing children working in factories shocked him and made him reconsider his career choices. He loves his work, so he didn't want to change career, but the experience made him consider more deeply the companies he chose to work for and who supplied their equipment.

My job doesn't meet my values.

You may have had times at work when you felt some of your values were met but other values weren't, or worse, your values were being heavily compromised. This is when you must ask yourself which values are most important to you. Rating your values in order of importance can help you understand what you will stand for when your values feel compromised and what you're prepared to put up with. As the saying goes, you must 'pick your battles'. Matthew put it this way:

> *"I try to be very environmentally conscious, but I work for companies that essentially rip trees out of the ground, turn them into stuff [kitchens], and then sell*

them for money. It's pure consumerism and capitalism, and it has its ups and downs. From my perspective, as a designer, you should have a consciousness responsibility to whatever you design; is this the right thing to do in the grand scheme of things? Am I using the right sustainable materials?" Matthew.

Matthew brings his values of sustainability into his work by consciously working to make sustainable choices in his designs. They don't always play out in the way he hoped, but he does his best to get sustainability onto the agenda.

Matthew loves his work, but he recognizes that it doesn't always live up to his values of sustainability. However, in terms of what matters to him right now, with a young family in tow and doing work he enjoys, he's learning while he works, and he feels somewhat happy to compromise that missing value for other values that matter more to him at this time.

In certain situations, you may find that some of the values you thought weren't as important to you will suddenly become more noticeable in specific situations. This can happen if you feel that part of what makes you unique is being threatened. In this scenario, you may have to rethink the ordering of your values. Listen to your heart and head and remember to consider the impact that your decisions could have on your longer-term goals.

What should you do if you find yourself in the wrong job, but you took it because it paid well? Michelle is a chartered psychologist and serial entrepreneur; this was her experience:

"My last proper job, on paper, was ideal, but it was difficult to do because there wasn't any budget or mandate for projects. I tried [to find other tasks to do instead of my defined role], but then I realized that none of these things were fulfilling me Eventually, I decided to quit. I cut my losses and left. There are always other opportunities." Michelle.

Sometimes, you have to assess your long-term goals and values and decide whether the short-term discomfort is worth it. If you decide it is, then it's important to find ways to mitigate some of the negative consequences by reframing tasks to help them better align to your values.

"During the 2008/9 recession, I was working [as an organizational psychologist in recruitment], and recruitment stopped. I found myself processing payroll and expenses just to give me something to do, and it was mind numbing. However, I decided to shift my focus away from the monotony of the job until the situation improved. To make my days more interesting, I'd make up stories about what people spend their expenses on. I was a chartered occupational psychologist, and I was doing expenses,

but I had a job, so I was grateful for the money and the organization. I loved working there, so it is all about reframing." Michelle.

Values bring purpose.

It's possible for any job, whatever tasks you are doing, to become purposeful by incorporating what you value. Ask yourself the following questions:

- How could I perform these tasks in a way that resonates with my values?

- How can I work on these tasks with someone else who aligns with my values or inspires me?

- How could I alter my role to do more of what I enjoy?

- How could I adjust these tasks to have a more concrete impact on the customers I serve so that they align with my values?

You have the power to realize your financial and personal goals.

Sometimes, you have to put your income needs first, but you can still find ways to be yourself while making that income. People who love what they do shape their work into something that drives them, and they aren't afraid to leave a job or situation if they feel it doesn't meet their needs. Elizabeth likes working for a company that gives her the freedom to run a project however she thinks is best.

"I can mold [my job] into what I enjoy as long as I have the autonomy to do so. The minute I don't [have that autonomy], I'll probably leave the job for something else." Elizabeth.

Doing what you love while making an income isn't easy. There are constant pulls on your energy to make the income you need to support yourself and your family. However, there are many ways you can shape your job or career into one that fulfills you, and those intentional decisions over the days, months, and years can ultimately lead you to doing work that you love.

You can find more on how to reshape your job into once that fulfils you in Part 3, How You Can Love Your Work.

Your money and passion balance may change.

Initially, the income we make is important to almost all of us, since most of us work to enable us to live. However, as you grow in your career, and if you're doing something that drives you, your desires may become more about fulfilling your passion than making an income.

Stuart is the founder of a building services company, but he spent much of his early career working as a building services engineer before he decided to branch out on his own.

Sophie is a co-founder of Roleshare, a smart matching site that helps people find jobs they can share with other professionals. The goal is to allow people to continue working in professional roles but with fewer hours. Sophie didn't start her career in the entrepreneurial space; she had roles at companies like Facebook and eBay in everything from technology and marketing to HR.

Stuart and Sophie both shared with me how their priorities have shifted throughout their careers and how financial gain can become secondary:

"My approach to income has changed over the last couple of years; before, my aim would have been to progress up the ranks and work on different projects, earning good money. But when we set up our own company, my priorities changed; they became more about being established in the field of work and helping others." Stuart.

"I think the financial aspect was very important, up to a certain point, and then I reached a place where I was happy with where I was. From there, my priorities focused more on opportunities for strategic impact and meaning. They changed throughout my life. Income is now more important again because I'm self-funding a start-up. Assuming that I'll find myself content again,

sustaining my lifestyle, my comfort, and all of those things, strategic impact and finding meaning from my work will become more important to me." Sophie.

Maurice, an IT Transformational Program Director & IT Project Manager, consciously chooses work that is relevant to where he wants his career to go, but he knows that he would take whatever work is on offer to support his family should the need arise.

"As much as I enjoy the work I do, I do it to provide for my family so we can enjoy being together and, you know, have a nice life. I wouldn't want to go out and actively seek something that was contrary to where my career was going, but if it came down to it, if it was between that and not having any money coming in, I would do it, because when you form a family unit, that is a very strong motivator." Maurice.

Even in dire circumstances, what is on offer for Maurice would likely be aligned, in some way at least, with what he loves to do and what he is good at because he has mindfully shaped his career and honed his skills in a direction that is important to him and what he loves. Therefore, people tend to seek him out for what he's known to be good at and enjoys. However, that position has taken years of mindful decisions to shape the path that works for him, much like all my other interviewees.

Whether it's adjusting how, when, or who you work with in your current job, planning your exit strategy for a new job, or starting a business alongside your regular job, there's always a way to balance your income and personal goals. However, to do so, you must continually make intentional decisions to do things that you value and enjoy most, while keeping your financial goals in mind. Remember, it's your career, and you own it. If it's not working for you, what can you do today to make a difference?

CHAPTER 5
FINDING WHAT
DRIVES YOU

"When I was a kid, I wanted to be an archaeologist. I really liked studying cultures and history, and I thought hieroglyphics looked really cool. I was about nine when I first saw them, and I thought that it would be the coolest thing to understand them. In some way, it's kind of interesting how I've come full circle, because I'm now working on coding languages." Maria.

After working as a restaurant server for years, making very little income, Maria stumbled upon coding as a potential career path. I say 'stumbled'; it was initially her husband who was looking for a new career, and he had tried 'free code camp' but hated it. He suggested that his wife should try it because he felt she might enjoy it. She is now a full stack developer and loves her new job and the good income it provides her and her family. More about Maria later.

This is often the way people develop careers they love. They are stuck doing something they don't enjoy, and they are sure there is nothing else out there for them, then a family member or friend or random situation makes them rethink and try something new.

Michelle grew up in Northern Ireland in the 1980s during the IRA bombings. She went through high school fascinated by why people do what they do. After watching a UK TV show called Cracker, about a forensic psychologist (someone who 'catches bad guys!'), she decided that was where she wanted to take her career. However, after taking strides to make her dream a reality, she found that the job wasn't what she'd seen on tv, so she changed course. She decided to train to be in the army, following in her father's footsteps, but when writing her dissertation, she researched the factors that make soldiers more stressed at work. She realized she could help people with her workplace knowledge, so she pivoted again to train to become an organizational psychologist. She now runs her own business in selection, recruitment, and assessment. What struck me about Michelle's story is how she linked her work and business back to her purpose. As a recruitment and employee selection specialist, Michelle helps organizations find the people who are the best fit for their culture. Effectively, she ensures companies don't recruit new people who might be a poor cultural or skills based fit. She keeps 'the bad guys' out.

"I was lying on the floor in a Bedwin tent in a church in London that had been bombed by the IRA. I was at a retreat about finding your 'why', and it all came to me in a flash. I realized that I help organizations keep bad guys out! Despite me not being TV's Cracker and not working with the police, I still catch bad guys and stop them joining organizations and causing mayhem! It was a fairly recent revelation I suppose, but I do catch bad guys; I got there in the end!" Michelle.

Sophie's current purpose and drive in her work comes, in part, from her passion to explore how various elements of businesses work:

"What I love about what I do is that it allows me to have my hands in many different parts of the business, learning and developing things that I never would have imagined I would even come across. I'm able to impact [the Roleshare technology platform we're building] and do things in a start-up that I would not have been able to do at a big company, simply because I wasn't trained in that area. It could have taken me quite a long time to get to that level of experience, but in a start-up, everyone has to have their hands in everything." Sophie.

Her passion to explore how to build a business is only part of what drives her. It is her mission to create workplaces where people can work more flexibly, including giving herself the same opportunity, which is a large part of what drives her. Her job at Roleshare also gives her the chance to use her technology skills and apply them in ways to do good for the wider community. Sophie's story is an example of how you can do what drives you on many levels and in different ways even in only one job role. More on Sophie's work later.

What is purpose?

Many times, I hear people say to those who are unhappy at work, 'you need to find your purpose!'. Hearing this always makes me cringe slightly because I find the phrase far too ethereal. It sounds like you're looking for something that is going to change the world. Not only is that a tremendously huge task, it's also almost impossible. I much prefer the phrases, 'what makes your blood boil?' or 'what do you find yourself getting lost in?'. These questions are much easier to answer, and they provide more actionable outcomes.

Questions like these help you realize that your purpose doesn't have to be something huge. In fact, your 'purpose' may be born from the fact that it makes your blood boil that you can never afford to take your family on vacation, so, currently, your primary goal is to make enough income to allow you to do just that. Alternatively, or once your primary goal is met, your 'purpose' may be something as large as mine, which is to change the world of work!

Your purpose matters to you, and the way you go about making that purpose a reality is aligned to your goals and how you see the world. It's also important to recognize that your purpose can change as often as you like, and you can have more than one. Perhaps your purpose is to earn enough money to take your family on vacation while also incorporating your baking passion into your work.

That's why listing your values in order of importance is so vital. It allows you to see what's most pressing and where you need to focus your energy, but it also helps you see that the priority of your values can easily change over time. Nothing is set in stone.

Perhaps you're single now; five years from now, you may have a family to raise and support. Your goals may well change, or they may not, but being clear about the mark (or marks) you want to make on the world, or on your family or your life, is the first step to doing what you love. The following quotes illustrates the different types of purpose and how they play out for each of us in different ways at different times in our lives. This is how Maurice sees his purpose of providing for and being present with his family:

> *"Family has an impact on whether I'd want to work for long periods abroad. When I worked abroad before, we had a family with three kids, and, actually, it was much easier [on the kids when I wasn't around] because it was a big buzzing family life, [so I wasn't*

as missed]. But two of our kids are at university now; there's only one at home, and if I was to work away, I think he would suffer a lot more because he'd have less interaction with people. As a result, I'm considering getting a job in London and going home in the evenings to catch up with him a bit more." Maurice.

Finding purpose.

Knowing your values is a good first step, but, often, finding out what you value is much more of an endeavor than just answering a few questions. Nadia and many of my other interviewees found their purpose through long-term self-reflection.

"That sense of purpose that I have has come through reflection and self-discovery, allowing me to think about what's important to me and what I can stand by. I want every young child to feel like they can live the life they want to live and not feel pressured to be someone they're not. I want that for every person in the world. I can't say that I'm able to touch every person in the world with what I do, but overall, that's my purpose ... It's not about pay, it's not about salary. My work within inclusive schools is not paid at the moment. We spent a whole year setting up this program, and it's all been voluntary. We've given so much of our time and we haven't been paid for it, but it's still work. I've still got a goal that I'm hoping to obtain, an

impact I'm hoping to have on society, on children, on people's lives, on something that's important to me."
Nadia

Nadia still works full time making a living to help support her family, but she ensures she makes time to work on her passion too.

While working at Facebook, Sophie was exposed to technology and how technology can help business ideas to scale. She loved her job, but she also had a goal in mind that she wanted to fulfil, so her purpose has changed over time.

"I was volunteering once a week while working crazy hours in marketing and advertising. I met a woman who was more senior than I was. She was also volunteering once a week but had fairly young twin boys. I remember asking her, 'How are you balancing this? You're putting me to shame, you know.' She replied, and I remember this very clearly, 'I'm very lucky that I share my job'. Sophie.

Job sharing is when two people share one job role. They split the hours and responsibilities, and they work as a team to meet the demands of the job.

"I had never heard that this was even a possibility. Ever since then, I had it at the back of my mind that this is such an interesting working model." Sophie.

That 'interesting working model' has now become the foundation for the startup that she and her husband formed, called 'Roleshare.' Roleshare is a technology platform that brings skilled professionals together so that they can divide full time job roles but only work on a part time basis. Off the back of her experience at Facebook and other companies working in technology, marketing, and advertising, while reflecting on her experiences and desires, she applied her knowledge, partnered with her husband, and put her dream into practice. She built a company that uses her skills gained through her various job roles to fuel her passion for creating workplaces that give people better balance between work and home life.

Stuart also has a life-altering purpose. He has a desire to shift the building services industry. Stuart shared a story with me about a project he worked on to encourage more graduates into the engineering industry. The project leader's plan was to use buildings like the iconic Shard in London to show graduates what they might get to work on. In reality, working on a world-renowned building as a building services engineer is rare. His goal as part of his career is to represent the industry in its truth; that it is more likely that you will work on unknown buildings. He wants people to understand that fulfillment as a building services engineer comes from doing engaging work helping to build structures like hospitals, schools, and elder care facilities. His aim is to encourage people into the industry who genuinely want to be there for the real work, not for the celebrity status. Rather than being part of institutions that are encouraging people into the industry through false messaging, he delivers talks to schools and universities about the real impacts of the building trade without the support of such institutions. He wants people to come into the industry with their eyes open and do the work simply because they enjoy it.

"The institutes and their staff are often just there to benefit themselves and don't necessarily think about the bigger picture. [Unfortunately,] trying to change anything in the industry we're currently in is like trying to turn an oil tanker; very slow and very difficult, because it's sort of an old boys' club, stuck in the ways of how things used to be." Stuart.

Despite change being a difficult thing to enact, Stuart doesn't give up, nor does he spend his days trying to alter the industry in a direct sense. He uses his time doing what he enjoys: working in the engineering industry and building his business. But in the background of that, he uses education to further a purpose that matters to him, representing the industry in its truth and bringing passionate new graduates into the field because they are interested in the trade itself. When the opportunity arises, he drives that purpose forward.

How can you find your purpose?

Throughout the following activity, we'll explore your current situation by answering the following questions:

- What do you like about your work now?

- What don't you like about your work now?

- What would you like to do more of?

- What would you like to do less of?

- How can you reframe your current situation?

Over the next week, record how you feel while completing your work tasks.

Each time you're working on something new, record how it makes you feel.

You can do this using a pen and paper, on your phone, or on your computer, wherever is most accessible to you.

Consider the following questions:

- What is the task?

- How does it make you feel? (Happy, frustrated, energized, irritable?)

- Do you currently feel under pressure? If so, why?

- Do you feel you have the skills needed to do the task well?

At the end of the week, look back at your record and see when you've had positive experiences and when you've had times of frustration.

Sometimes, especially if you're in a job that you feel you hate, you can get bogged down in believing every part of that job is negative. However, when you record what you're feeling at different points in the day, you may start to see that certain parts of your job are more enjoyable than others.

You can also compare your answers for each task to see where there are similarities and differences. You might find that the reason you enjoy one type of task is also why you like another task and that, actually, the reason you like the task isn't because of the task per-se but because of the impact it's having on someone or something else.

The process of focusing on what you do, why you do it, and how you do it helps you to see more objectively what is working for you and what is not. This focus can help you see what ultimately drives you in your work.

Building purpose within your role.

Your 'purpose' could be centered around something that matters to you within your daily role, rather than something that has a bigger impact on society. For example, Maurice is aware that, sometimes, the companies he works for worry that consultants don't understand the depth of their organizational issues. Part of his purpose is making sure that the people he works for don't feel that way.

"I always take a step back to ask myself, 'am I actually helping to move the organization forward? Am I doing something that is actually adding value?'" Maurice.

For Elizabeth, part of her purpose is being able to be true to herself, working on things that interest her, and doing the things she's good at. Her work allows her to express herself and her passions in ways she can't do at home.

"I would not be able to function without work. [How I am at work is] totally different to how I am at home, to a degree. The skills I use and the role I have at work are different, and I really thrive on those things. I like going to work and I like doing my job. If I have any personal struggles, works always keeps me grounded." Elizabeth.

Deciding between need and purpose.

"If you pick a job that you enjoy, something you're passionate about, it doesn't feel like work. It's a vocation; it almost becomes a hobby." Stuart.

For some of us, work can provide fulfillment to the point where it no longer feels like 'work'. We spend time searching for a job role as a source of satisfaction rather than a means to an end. For others, work is all about making an income.

Denny and Lia went into their careers thinking money was the key to success.

"What was really driving my choice of career was the financial gains. I was looking into which different careers make a lot of money. But then I realized I didn't really enjoy the work. I realized that [money] was not actually going to be an avenue to happiness." Denny.

Denny decided to pivot from a career that he knew would make money to a career that interested him. He chose to work as a consultant, helping to guide employees through organizational change. He didn't know if there was going to be a good income in his choice, but he knew it inspired him and he wanted to learn more.

Lia followed a path from school to university to a role delivering corporate training to employees in the finance industry. After a few years, Lia felt unfulfilled and left her corporate training job to start her own business. She has built her business to provide her with multiple income streams, from helping teenagers write their college applications to her true passion of inspiring and enhancing the life of seniors, particularly those with dementia. Lia spends her time creating and delivering training and development programs that help these seniors to have meaningful social interactions and improve the quality of their lives.

Lia doesn't earn the big salary she had in her corporate role, but she loves her work and she decided that was more important to her. Her work is filled with both challenging and inspiring moments, and these moments are what drive her to give her best to her work.

"I was once doing a talk [at an elder care home] and a woman [with advanced dementia] unbuttoned her shirt, took it off, and said, 'This is my bra'. I had to roll with it, because for her that was important to share. You don't want to laugh, and you don't want to embarrass people. Many of the I've met people in elder care communities have PhDs and had very successful careers. I want to bring awareness to the fact that they still deserve to be treated as valuable members of society; they still deserve to have dignity in social interactions. But more than that, they deserve to have social interactions that are meaningful, and that's what I aim to bring to elder care communities." Lia.

Making your job work for you.

Working for money is always going to be important to most of us, and it would be naïve to advise choosing passion over money if you need that money for your family. However, finding or creating opportunities at work that allow you to earn the income you need while simultaneously enjoying at least some of the work you do is where the magic happens. It doesn't have to be one or the other. Here are a few ways you can begin to include the things that bring you joy into your work:

- Volunteer for projects in areas you enjoy.

- Craft your job to make it what you enjoy. More on role crafting in Chapter 12.

- Learn about other areas that interest you, and reshape your work by using some of your new skills.

- Try new things, keeping track of what you like and don't like, and why, through journaling.

"One of the things I do, and I have always done, is journaling. I find that journaling has really helped me reflect. [I'm] very honest with myself when I'm journaling, and I have found that it has been quite helpful in guiding me on my decisions and my vision of things that I want to achieve." Sophie.

When you begin to shape what you do, you *become* that shape; it takes on a life of its own, as people come to you to ask you to do the things you never thought you'd be known for.

When one of my interviewees, Emily, was working as a bar manager in London UK, she recognized that there were elements of her job that she really enjoyed that she wasn't getting the chance to do as often as she liked. Therefore, she sought out those opportunities outside of her job, and then, as people gave her those jobs and she practiced her skills, she began to become known for her abilities in those areas.

Two of those areas were writing drinks menus and marketing the products on the bar. She subsequently shaped her future career around writing and marketing.

When Emily was working in London, freelancing for a woman called Kirsty, who was just starting a business, she loved that she could get involved in all aspects of the business and learn the ropes. However, as time passed, she met her partner and wanted to move away to the country to start a family. Her purpose changed, and she knew she would need to change her lifestyle to fit with that. However, she wasn't starting her family right away, and, when she did move, she missed her work in London. She decided to adjust her working hours and commute to the city a few days a week to allow her to live the best of both worlds. Once she got pregnant a couple of years later, she changed things again and left her London job. However, the transition felt easier because she had gradually made the change.

"We were both ready for new things when I was pregnant. I just didn't feel like I could keep working in such an intensively drink-based industry when I would have a young child to get home to every night. By that stage, Kirsty [my manager] had an office and a sales

force, not just one or two people. She had a proper business, and she wasn't as reliant on just one person anymore." Emily.

Adjusting your job into one that works for you isn't always an easy path; it takes time and constant self-reflection to adjust and decide the right course for you. It can also mean putting yourself into scenarios that feel risky or unsettling but that help you develop new skills and new career perspectives.

"I was determined not to do what many of my friends did, falling into whichever job was available. I wanted to find my own way. I found a furniture maker, who I worked with for two years. At the same time, I set up my own [furniture design business] and got stuck in with the arts crowd in Sheffield. I worked doing that for two years, loved it, and learned an awful lot more than I ever had at uni. I learned more in that two-year period running a business [than I did at university] with literally no money but having a great time doing it." Matthew.

What drove Matthew was finding his own way. When Emily was a bar manager, she made a point of working on tasks outside of her expected job role so that she could explore what she enjoyed.

"I knew [working as a bar manager] wasn't forever. It was like a placeholder job, but there were aspects

of it that I really enjoyed. I loved creating cocktail lists, working with brands, learning about the stories behind the brands, and running training sessions for the team. When I had a bar team that was starting to flag, because it was a busy season, I'd get someone in for something like tequila training. You knew your staff would have a good time, and you knew they'd relax and bond as a team but also learn something that they could then pass on to the customers at the bar. Exploring tasks that interested me and digging deeper into the marketing side of the business (even though that wasn't in my job description) was how I started to learn what I liked about marketing." Emily.

When you find your true calling.

I first met Yasmin when she was 25. We were both studying for a graduate diploma course in psychology. Yasmin wasn't sure which path she wanted to take at the end of her course, but she had an interest in psychology and wanted to explore it further. At the end of the diploma course, Yasmin decided to apply for a further graduate qualification to train to become a therapist. She didn't get in because she lacked experience. She was devastated, and she started to question if it was what she genuinely wanted to do as a career. Over the next few years, she explored her options.

"I worked in a school for a year with children, which helped me realize that I wanted to work with adults. I then worked in social services for a bit. My mom's cousin got me an administrative job in an office down the road from me that hires rooms to therapists to hold their sessions with clients. I came across a lot of therapists and psychologists who were renting rooms, and I remember chatting to them. It really sparked my interest again. I realized that passion I had." Yasmin.

After years of exploring and finding that her true calling was exactly where she'd felt it was originally, she began a 5-year course, training to become a therapist. She worked part-time to pay for her studies, and she qualified in 2020. She couldn't be happier with her choice.

Sometimes, you need to veer off track to recognize what you really want. And when you find what you want, it's up to you to decide whether the risks involved in creating that career are worth taking.

Lia's experience of moving from a job in corporate America to her true passion of working with people in elder care homes and helping educate people with dementia reflects what is possible when you want to reshape your career. She built her business from scratch in a field in which no-one seemed to be doing the work she was doing. She did so because the close relationship she had with her grandmother inspired her to help others in the elder care community:

"I stepped so far out of my comfort zone into such an unfamiliar world [in terms of work], but I truly believe I've always fitted in here." Lia.

Anyone can build a career they love. It may not happen quickly, and it may be due to very small steps over a long time, but anyone can do it. When you logically plan how to bring your passions to life, even in the smallest ways, while also ensuring you're meeting your financial needs, you too can build a career you love.

CHAPTER 6
SEEKING BALANCE
TO YOUR DAYS

One of the most interesting conversations I've had since I started this research was with a nurse during an unexpected dawn visit to the Emergency Room. The nurse seemed tired, and I initially felt sorry for him being on the night shift. I said to him, "it must be hard working here through the night. I don't think I could do what you do". He told me that the night shift was his preferred choice because it allowed him to work with the 'more fun' members of the team, it paid much better than the day shift, and it was when the 'interesting things' happen!

When I hear stories like this, I am reminded of the diversity that exists in career choices. The thought of working a night shift in an Emergency Room is my idea of hell, and yet this nurse thrived on it.

When, where, and how we work has become more prominent than ever. The pandemic has shone a light on everyone's working days and has encouraged many to reconsider the design of their working schedules. The balance of your day is personal to you, though it is likely to change over time. One of the key factors that arose when talking to people who love their work was finding a balance to suit their needs.

People who love to work are intentional about the way they want to work, the hours they want to work, and how they want to use those hours.

When and where you work.

What I've found interesting since doing my research is how much I feel that my research emulates what we see in the news about the changing state of our working lives. There is a desire for more choice and flexibility in work that wasn't there before. We are recognizing that, for many, the 9–5 day, or a day of structured hours, doesn't allow us to meet the demands of modern family life. Many want to be able to take their children to and from school, care for elderly parents, or squeeze in a gym session before work. Others don't want lengthy commutes. However, I often hear from friends, family, and colleagues about the divide between those who want to work remotely and those who want to work on site or in offices. The variation of preference is huge, and there is definitely no one approach that works for everyone.

Many people crave and thrive on structure in their working lives. They like to know what time they'll start work, where they need to be during the day, what tasks are required of them, and what time they can clock out. These people may well feel that their time is respected, so they will give more of themselves while they are at work and take breaks when they need them, coming back fresh the following day.

While I am a big promoter of flexible working opportunities, and I believe they are a necessity for modern day workplaces, some people prefer the structure of working in an office.

> *"I'm crap at working from home. I could work, but take me out of the office environment and I'm just distracted by what's on the radio or I start organizing the Lego by size and color. I'm not great at working from home. But also, being stuck behind a desk is not my idea of fun. Getting up and about, looking at stuff and going places, or building something, going to someone else's department and catching up—those are the really good bits."* Matthew.

However, 'structure' doesn't require 9–5 hours of work. People who love their work have a structure that works for them, and they have found organizations or ways of working that support their flexible needs:

> *"I have worked as a freelancer since I was about 28. I had a full-time job as well back then and took on lots of extra client work alongside the full-time job. When I had my second child, I dropped the full-time*

job. Raising two children is like a full-time job in itself. A 'bums on seats' 9–5 job in an office with somebody watching the clock wasn't going to suit our family." Emily.

The key to a happy work life is finding what works for you and finding a company or a work life that will encourage and support you to work in a way that is most productive and appealing for your circumstances. Of course, you may find yourself in a situation where you are so in need of a job that you can't go hunting for a specific company or a specific job; you have to take what you can get. While this may be true, having a job doesn't mean you can't keep looking for the right role or keep learning about what will work better for you. The secret to building a happy work life is never, never, never giving up.

Lia shared with me that she believes her "circadian rhythms are broken". She finds it incredibly difficult to wake up before 10am, and she finds she does her best work in the evenings and into the early hours of the morning. Working to such a pattern was challenging for her when she worked in her corporate job, so when she finally branched out to work for herself, she felt she could thrive:

"I found a way to not be a morning person and have a more successful life than I ever had when I worked in a [corporate job]. I'm also so much happier because

I'm not pressuring my body to do something that doesn't work for it." Lia.

Sometimes, we require different schedules altogether to allow us space to branch off into something new. Often, when people set up their own businesses, the idea of having no regular income is scary, so they want to work part time in their current job and part time on their business.

"When I first set up my business, I started working part-time at the NHS as an Occupational Psychologist for Northumbria Healthcare Trust. I went from being a strategic recruitment manager to just doing psychometric testing. But that was brilliant because it was only three days a week. It was half my last salary, but it gave me stability, income, and awesome colleagues." Michelle.

Flexible working opportunities allow us to integrate work and home life.

In the past, the discussion around flexible working mostly focused on people who needed to be available for their children. More recently, society is recognizing that flexible working opportunities can be useful and desirable for people with and without children, those who have caring responsibilities for other family members or friends, and people who have either physical or mental health problems. In short, we're realizing that we shouldn't necessarily have to fit our lives outside of work around our work demands, but that we should have the option to shape our full lives in ways that work for us while we make a living.

In the past, 'taking holiday' or 'having a break' also encompassed people taking time out for important elements in their life; elements that are far from vacations. This can include circumstances in people's lives that are unavoidable and challenging and occasions when people require more flexibility.

Thankfully, more flexible working options are beginning to be seen as necessary for good mental health and as one of the major factors contributing to more efficient, productive, and successful workers and organizations.

Unfortunately, there is a still a long way to go before flexible working opportunities become the norm.

Many organizations still believe in the idea that you need to be present in an office or on site to be doing your work effectively. Many employers also practice 'presenteeism', which means being present at work even when you're sick. For many jobs, being present in an office or on site for a full day isn't necessary. Being present when they're sick can be detrimental to a worker's health or the health of those around them. Many jobs have the option for people to work remotely and outside traditional working hours. The issues arise when organizations believe that people can't be trusted to do their best work when they are not tied to strict structures. To be most effective, managers and leaders need to adapt to measure success on the work achieved rather than the time present at work.

Making flexible working the norm and not a 'nice to have' is about changing attitudes so that people feel comfortable to be wherever they need to be or want to be while working around the requirements of their job roles.

In some jobs, being present is necessary, but that doesn't take away the option of creating shared job roles to allow people more flexibility. Giving people the choice to work in the way that works for them is one of the keys to happier workers and more productive workplaces. My research has shown me that, when people have agency over how, when, and where they work, if they wish to have those choices, their engagement improves, and they are more likely to find joy in their work.

You have choices.

Many people feel that they don't have the choice but to work the way they are told to work. I've met countless people who feel stuck in careers they hate, with no idea of how to change their situation. I spent a lot of time believing that was just the way work was. As time went on and I saw people build fulfilling careers, I realized that this *isn't* the way things have to be. One of my interviewees confirmed this realization and gave me hope that change is possible for anyone.

Maria, who was nearly 30 at the time, had been home-schooling her four kids, but she wasn't really enjoying it and she craved something more than her part-time job as a waitress at Olive Garden. Her husband was working away as a trucker, and she wanted him to come home, but they knew they couldn't survive on her waitressing wages. In the past, her husband had tried Free Code Camp, a free resource that allows you to try out coding as a potential career path, but realized he didn't enjoy it. However, as they were looking for a solution to their predicament, he suggested his wife try it to see if it appealed to her. She enjoyed it from the first lesson and went on to complete her 9-month Free Code Camp course in her limited free time, and then she started a course at Flatiron School.

I asked her how she managed to fit her coding training into her schedule.

"Getting through Flatiron School was really tough because I had all the kids with me. From February to July, I was at home by myself while my husband was trucking. I would get up and homeschool the kids, and I would run the household until about three o'clock. Between three to five, I would code, and then from about five, we would eat dinner, I would play with the kids, and then they'd go to bed about eight o'clock. From about eight o'clock to midnight, I would code. I didn't do it every night because I still was working

at the restaurant. I did it about two or three nights a week, so it was very slow going." Maria.

'Slow going' is probably an understatement with so much going on in her life, but she made the time to educate herself because she wanted a different career. She also used all of the free resources she could find to give herself a kickstart before taking on formal training a year or so later.

What kind of day works for you?

Matthew was happy with his working day until he had his first child. He struggled to find the flexibility he wanted and was frustrated at the fact that his colleagues and managers didn't understand the difficulties he was facing.

"When we had the first born, I was working with a team of people who'd had either had kids a long time ago or didn't have any at all. My manager was also new and didn't have kids, so he didn't really get it. He didn't understand the kind of flexibility I needed. That was why I eventually had to move to a different department in the business." Matthew.

Matthew had to think carefully about what he needed from his work while also meeting the needs of his family.

The key to a creating a happier and more productive day is figuring out what kind of working day works best for you.

Activity

Answer the 11 questions below to help you to decide if you're someone who likes a more structured day set by someone else, a structured day set by you, or a less structured day in which you can come and go as you please. Answer every question with the following scale:

① Strongly disagree

② Disagree

③ Neither agree nor disagree

④ Agree

⑤ Strongly agree

Remember, whatever you choose, you still have deadlines to meet to deliver your work. The pressures don't go away, but you can decide how you'd rather do them and when. Having control over your day, or being the agent of your own career, is one of the secrets to loving what you do.

- I like to be to home at the same time every day to have dinner with my family.
- I want to be able to leave work a few hours early for my child's sports game (If you don't have children, imagine another activity you would like to attend on a weekly or bi-weekly basis.)
- I dislike commuting.

- I can concentrate on my work in a coffee shop, library, or other public space that isn't a defined office or work site.
- I see myself as self-motivated.
- I feel comfortable using technology to connect with others.
- I would happily work late at night if I had to meet a deadline.
- I feel confident deciding how to prioritize my work.
- I can stop myself from being distracted by home tasks that require my attention.
- I draw my energy from being in quiet spaces. Being around other people drains my energy.
- I have or I can create a comfortable physical work set up at home.

If you scored between 55-44, you are probably someone who would thrive in a flexible working scenario. You would love the opportunity to manage your own day and come and go as you please, fitting work in around your schedule. You wouldn't mind working into the night to meet a deadline if it meant you were able to attend your child's music recital or have dinner with friends.

If you scored between 23-43, you would likely prefer a hybrid working model. This means you would like some time in an office or on-site and other time working from home or in other locations. You like to have the flexibility to do things you enjoy outside of work, but you also like some of the structure of specific times you need to be at your workplace. You might like the opportunity to work, say, three days in the office and two days from home, or vice versa.

If you scored between 0-22, you likely love the structure of working on-site surrounded by your colleagues. You like the camaraderie of having people around every day, and you like the structure of starting and finishing work at scheduled times. You prefer to fit your life around your structured work schedule rather than fitting work around the rest of your life.

Once you have a clearer picture of the working style that best suits you, you can try to find a way to shape your career to meet those needs. This may not be a quick fix; it can take time to reshape your work to meet your needs, but you can make small steps towards those changes each day.

Making flexible schedules work for you and your employer.

Employers often feel they need to give employees the chance and freedom to prove that they are capable of working flexibly. Showing how you plan to achieve the tasks required of you is an important step towards creating the trust relationship required between you and your managers and team members that will make your flexible working patterns effective. If you can achieve more than what's required, it will likely persuade your employer to make flexible working a reality. However, don't fall into the trap of feeling that you must work longer and harder because you have been granted some freedom to work on your schedule. Ultimately, you're still delivering the work that is required of you for the salary you receive. Remember to respect your boundaries about what you believe is fair to deliver (in line with your role expectations) without burning yourself out.

Another factor to consider is that flexibility can come with increased responsibility. Deciding whether you're ready to take that on is an important step in determining if a more flexible working schedule will suit your lifestyle. You can seek out some flexibility initially but accepting how much you can handle when structuring your own day and work-load is something to consider before looking for a completely flexible schedule.

How to request a flexible working day

If you decide a flexible working pattern is best for you, here are some tips for how you can request flexible working arrangements from your employer:

- Explain to your employer how they can measure your work success regardless of how often you're present in the office or on-site. This may include:

  o Providing deadlines for specific projects.

  o Setting regular check-ins to show progress on your work or to ask questions.

  o Showing how you will connect with colleagues when not meeting face-to-face.

  o Explaining how often and where you will schedule face-to-face meetings with other colleagues, if necessary.

  o Explaining how you will report back to your manager on your progress with your work.

- Explain to your manager why you need a flexible working schedule and the hours you need. Make the explanation beneficial for you and your manager. How is this a positive outcome for them? Perhaps you'll be working with less distractions or maybe you will have more time to concentrate on your work as you will reduce lengthy commutes.

- Clarify with your manager the work you have on your plate and propose to them how you will complete that work in the time that you have.

- Explain how you will meet with colleagues without being present in physical meetings:

    o What technologies will you use?

    o What times will the meetings be?

    o How long will the meetings last?

- How will you all keep track of what was discussed? Suggest or show evidence for technologies you could use. Provide evidence of what you've discussed with colleagues about how you can make your proposed flexible working patterns possible.

- Describe the benefits of flexible working to you and your colleagues, e.g., everyone can attend necessary or desired appointments without taking time off. You could show that there will now always be someone available to connect with colleagues and customers at different times of the day.

The way you work.

Flexible working isn't just about flexible hours; it's also about flexibility within your job role.

Whether working for themselves or for other organizations, every person I interviewed had some element of their work that was essential, or what one interviewee termed their 'bread and butter work'. This type of work was vital to pay the bills or meet the requirements of their job role. However, they shaped their careers to include other elements inside or outside their job roles, which furthered their careers, using elements of the vocation they enjoyed most. There are always specific tasks that *must* be done and done in a specific way – the bread-and-butter work – in a job role, but there is often space to explore new tasks or different ways of doing current tasks too.

> *"A lot of jobs, although they seem very structured, allow you to put your own stamp on them."* Maurice.

One of my interviewees wanted her work to better suit her personality, so she looked for a role that allowed her to work in the way *she* liked to work:

> *"I've always had jobs that are repetitive, where you just do the same thing every day: customer service jobs, sales jobs. I did telemarketing for a while, which bored me to death. A couple of years ago, I found out that*

I have high functioning autism, so I have a pretty busy mind. That's why I got into coding in the first place; I got a chance to create and make different things. I still used the same patterns [of coding language rules to follow], but I could [code creatively] every time. That was really one of the things that motivated me to keep going. Every day is different. It's not repetitive. It's not boring. I'm much happier with what I'm doing now." Maria.

Crafting your role to suit you.

'Job crafting' is a psychological concept that advocates employees having control over how they work, with particular focus on driving personal goals as well as business goals. While many companies struggle with the idea of employees furthering their personal goals while at work, people who are the most self-engaged in their work are those with self-imposed control or, as I like to call it, agency over their careers. They make sure they get their essential work done, but they look for interesting ways to do it. They also look for other things outside of their role that interest them. As long as those tasks also help to further the business, they are a win-win for employee and employer.

It's very easy to get stuck feeling that you can't shift the role you have into one you can enjoy, especially if you have been unhappy in that role for several years. It can also be difficult to live outside the structures created by an organization, because sticking to these structures are how you get rewarded for your work.

"I felt like I was becoming part of this big corporate machine, where I had to change how I did things in order to deliver and be successful in the eyes of the leadership. You know what you need to do, and you know how to do it, but you just start to get sucked into doing it only because you get rewarded for it. I would never take the time to deeply connect with anybody; it was more about taking the time to do what I needed to deliver." Bhavisha.

Bhavisha was unhappy in her role, but over time she noticed that, if you begin to work in a different way, people start to work differently around you.

By exploring her career and thinking about which needs she would like to see met at her work, she decided to use her training and insights in coaching and mentoring to inform how she and other managers work:

"I think what companies should improve on is understanding their individual staff a lot better. An unhappy person may not realize that they're actually missing a creative side to their role. They might actually be better off doing something in the digital world or working in marketing. I just don't think we do enough to under-

stand employees better and see if there is anything we can do to promote a more natural way of working." Bhavisha.

As a manager, Bhavisha started to think more deeply about how her team's roles are structured and whether those structures make for fulfilling work rather than only delivering what's required for the business. When people can do more of what they're good at and enjoy instead of sticking to specific job descriptions and required tasks, they become more engaged in their work. As long as the necessary tasks are done, you can be creative with who does what and how they do it.

Matthew, the product designer, brings his desire for using sustainable materials into his designs whenever feasible. Sophie, the co-founder of Roleshare, has combined her technology skills with her passion project of providing sharing roles to allow people to have more flexible working. They have all developed the role balance that works for them.

Other people manage to craft their roles in ways that work for them by taking on tasks that are outside of their role remit, and some find their work balance by starting side businesses or studying topics of interest. Meanwhile, others work as free-lancers, picking and choosing the jobs that best suit their skills and interests. However they manage their careers, people who love to work have found ways to balance the work they *need* to do with the work they *want* to do. There are many more ways to do this, and I challenge you to look for all the ways in which my interviewees have found this balance as you continue to work through the book.

Permission to take control.

It may be tough to find flexibility in your work without gently manipulating your situation. The goal is to give you more opportunities to do the tasks that interest you and/or work on the schedule that suits you best. However, without making the decision to shape your life *your* way, you will never achieve the fulfillment you want in your work.

You may be lucky and have a manager or team that look out for you and help you develop new skills; you may even have a good rapport with them. However, when the chips are down, most people will fend for themselves. If your company happens to be struggling financially, you can bet your bottom dollar the company won't think twice about making your job redundant if they have to. For this reason, having an exit strategy is also always a good idea. It's always helpful to hedge your bets.

When you constantly remind yourself that organizations exist to make money, you'll realize that the actions of the staff in the companies are often not personal. They come from the need to keep the company running.

Unfortunately, many companies don't recognize that, when employees feel supported, cared for, nurtured, and protected, they can thrive and make the company more profitable.

It's your future.

I truly believe a company should always support you, but your progress, development, and enjoyment at work is not only down to them. You have a responsibility to look after you and shape your career the way you want it to be.

Shaping your role to allow you to do the tasks that drive you is a big part of creating a future that makes your skills shine and makes you happy.

Lastly, if you are clear about what you're looking for to help you have a happier life through your work and you find your employer is not open to supporting you on that journey, remember there are always other options. There may not be another job out there right now, but nothing is stopping you from exploring ideas, learning new things, or looking for ways to reshape your current role. I'm not necessarily telling you to quit what you're currently doing; I am giving you the permission to explore other possibilities. It's your life, and it's always up to you to make it meet your needs.

CHAPTER 7
PRIORITIZING DEVELOPMENT

"I don't understand people who don't want to improve themselves. I'm all about improvement at work, and I'm very aware of my strengths and my flaws. I always want to be better." Elizabeth.

The question is: How do you find what you're prepared to sacrifice your free time to learn?

If you haven't found anything in your career that interests you, learning can seem all-consuming and boring and maybe even pointless. Who wants to learn about something that doesn't interest them? But when you find what you enjoy, digging deeper is exciting. You'll find you want to keep delving further and further and you're ready to give that topic much more of your time and energy.

In return, that work gives you time and energy back through the experience of psychological flow. Psychological flow is a concept that was coined by Mihaly Csikszentmihalyi. It's the feeling you get when you you're 'in the zone' or lost in the moment. Time passes without you realizing it, and once the activity you're doing is over, you look back and realize you very much enjoyed what you were doing. Flow comes when you are challenged but believe you can achieve the challenges laid out in front of you.

I'm a writer and I love writing. I love having power over which words to use and in which order to use them to convey meaning and insights that might not have been shared by others. I love the challenge of making the words form a melody so that they sing back to me and other readers from the page. But writing can sometimes frustrate me, and I'll find myself wanting to give up for one reason or another. Learning to be a good writer, like any skill, takes time, patience, time away from family, early mornings, research, commitment, drive, and patience. I experience self-doubt some days and self-belief other days, but I keep going, even when there are dips in productivity, because it matters to me.

Finding tasks that challenge you but give you that same joy I describe above will help you achieve a career you love. Although I must sacrifice some of the other things I enjoy doing to be able to write, I don't sacrifice what I enjoy for what I don't enjoy. I put my time into getting better at something that drives me, however difficult it gets at times. Bhavisha's flow experience comes from working on her side business:

"I don't care how busy I've been at work. I'll come home and actually really look forward to working on [my side business] at the end of the day, no matter how tired I am." Bhavisha.

Directing your own learning.

I'm always struck by how people who enjoy what they do manage to fit so much into their already busy lives. They do so because what they do gives them energy and opportunities to pivot in their career if they so wish.

"I don't only have my current job role. I'm also an internal auditor, a BPI practitioner, and a lead change maker and facilitator. I take on all these additional things to better myself and understand the business model better, but it also gives me more opportunities in case I want to move on to something else. I've built networks elsewhere and skills outside of work." Elizabeth.

"I coded at least every day and sometimes on the weekends. Every day, every night, no matter how I was feeling. Sometimes, I would have a migraine and I would still code. Sometimes, you just have to ignore your feelings and keep your focus on what you're doing and what your aim is." Maria.

When I first started working at a consulting firm at the beginning of my career, more senior colleagues used to say to me, "go and have coffee with the staff, go and meet other people". I used to think, as someone new and fresh to the consulting world, why do I have to do that? Why do I need to put myself in a situation in which I will feel uncomfortable and awkward?

As time went on, I realized it wasn't just about having coffee with a random person; it is important to spend time with other members of staff to get to know what they're doing and what they're working on. It's an opportunity to ask questions to see whether their role is something that interests you, if you have the same skills, or if there is mutual interest in a subject. It's about building relationships and looking for sparks of curiosity. I didn't see that when I started working because it felt like a transactional situation.

Eventually, I realized that making these connections, both with people and activities, was about shaping a career that I enjoyed and was good at. But it takes effort, time, and persistence, and it often requires you to put yourself in awkward or challenging situations to get where you want to be.

The thing about training and learning in organizations is that some of it may be interesting to you, but some of it may not. When you direct your own learning, you can dive into whichever rabbit holes pique your interest. You don't have to follow anyone else's defined path. That's when you find what really drives you and how you want to spend your time to grow and develop.

Finding what you enjoy takes work.

"You've probably been there at one point in your life, looking at jobs boards and thinking, what could I do? You'll discount jobs that you don't think you're good enough for or you think will bore you. Or perhaps you'll think you don't have the qualifications. I went through all of that. I asked people, 'what should I do?', and I realized the answer was about reconnecting with myself and rewinding, thinking, how do I find out what I was actually put on Earth to do?" Bhavisha.

I've lost count of the number of times someone has told me how they hate the job they landed but got there because they studied X at university. They fell into a job and don't know how to get themselves out of it. Many people spend hours trawling the internet looking for that perfect role but never find it. That's because, to find what you love, you must look within and build on your sparks of interest to create the career you love.

"When I started [painting] two years ago, I had no idea about technique or anything. I'm self-taught, so I watched videos and then just started with canvas and paper. I thought, 'Okay, I'm [going to be a good painter

or a bad painter]. After the first painting, I learned so much and I wanted to learn more and more. I worked really hard to reach where I am now. I think that's the key. If you really want something, you need to commit yourself to what you want to be. It just takes practice. That is the only way you're going to reach the level you want." Virginia.

You have so much time.

I spend on average four hours a day on my phone. Of course, that's in fits and starts, but it's my time all the same. What do I get from that? Very little. I have some work-related channels I use to help me to progress my business, but I often mindlessly scroll. It can cause jealousy, irritability, a sense of despair, and emptiness. They may sound like extreme emotions, but when you boil down how social media makes you truly feel and the impact it has on your time and life, it becomes clear that there are more constructive things you could be doing with your precious time to develop yourself, your career, and your world.

It's easy to become addicted to social media; so many of us make conscious efforts to spend time away from it. For me, that time away from social media is what propelled me to begin writing this book. I'd been talking about it for 5 years and had never taken the plunge. Listening to others and seeing others being successful made me doubt my abilities to achieve.

However, I realized that it doesn't matter what anyone else is doing. I also realized that what you see on social media or TV or in magazines focuses on those who've achieved success because they have been persistent in their work. They have found things that interest them, and they continually work at those things to become good at them. They have failed many times and picked themselves back up and started again.

When I'm not with my children and I'm not working, I get to choose what I do with my time. I constantly ask myself, will I waste my time on social media today or will I write?

Where does your time go?

Ask yourself the following questions to help you understand where your time goes and whether those activities are serving you:

1. What do you do with your *free* time? (Be honest and count everything!)

2. What do you get from the activities you do with your free time? What do they give you?

3. Why do you need these activities in your life? Are they useful to you? Are they necessary?

4. What would happen if you didn't engage in these things?

5. What would you do with your time if you didn't do the things you mention above?

Assessing what you do with your time can help you decide what you value most and whether to keep those things in your life or substitute them for other things. At the end of the day, it's your time and your life to do with however you choose. Of course, there will always be non-negotiable activities in life, but once you find what activities you enjoy and can help you grow, you may also discover ways to reshape those non-negotiables into activities that make you happier, help you develop skills that interest you, or help you move in the directions you want to go. Bhavisha shared these thoughts with me:

"Everyone has the same amount of time in the day. We have the same amount of time that Einstein had or Edison or Obama or Elon Musk. Every one of us has the same amount of time. Remember that when you see highly inspirational people. I'm not saying we all have to aim to be like them, but we all have the same amount of time in the day." Bhavisha

Finding your flow.

"The flow experience that results from the use of skills leads to growth; passive entertainment leads nowhere." Mihaly Csikszentmihalyi, FLOW.

We all have activities we enjoy more than others, but often, when people say 'do what you love' we think we need to make money out of our favorite hobbies. But doing what you love is much more nuanced than that. Many activities we do and enjoy are best left as hobbies.

"I enjoy cooking. But I'm a cook in a sea of people that are much better than me, much more experienced, who have a skill set. I do it for myself on my own." Lia.

Lia knows that she is good at cooking, and she knows that she enjoys it. Perhaps, with the right training, she could have been an excellent chef, but she clearly doesn't have the inclination to develop in that area. She recognizes that, even with the training, she doesn't believe she could compete with the top chefs. She doesn't see that path as a viable income source or one that would give her a fulfilled working life. It doesn't drive her or give her a chance at the financial rewards she desires, like other things in her life.

If you're considering using a skill you enjoy in your work, you must ask yourself: *Do I want to be good enough to make a living from this skill? Am I prepared to learn how to be good enough to compete in the marketplace?* If you are prepared for this, it's time to look at the steps you need to take to reach the level of skill necessary in the subject area that interests you.

If you follow that path, it's important to recognize that you don't necessarily have to be 'the best', you just have to find your market or audience. But to do that, you still must work at your chosen craft. But if the thought of the work doesn't excite you, it won't matter how good the dream of 'making it' in that area sounds, you won't ever 'make it' because those who do, continue to work on that craft even on days when they don't feel like it. If you don't love the craft, what will encourage you to keep going even on the bad days?

People who love to work love to learn; when you love what you do, you naturally want to become better at your craft. You love the challenge of continuing to learn while also feeling that you have enough knowledge that you already have something to offer. In a nutshell, you want to find your flow.

[I'm] always going to be learning, so I don't try to do it overnight. I don't even try to learn in only six months or a year. I take it slower and go deeper." Maria.

Virginia is a self-taught artist, and she loves painting. She knows that, to continue to grow in her craft, she needs to put herself in situations that feel uncomfortable and challenge her. She also knows that, once she has learnt a new skill, she can use it to enjoy more of her time painting as she continually achieves new heights and masters new challenges.

"When I want to create something, I push myself to accomplish. In that precise moment, I may not really enjoy it because I'm struggling with something new. But when I see the painting, I think, 'Now I know how to do this next time." Virginia.

Understanding what you enjoy is the foundation for knowing where to seek development opportunities. Knowing these things about yourself will help you find where you are likely to excel, feel most comfortable, and enjoy your work.

However, opportunities for development rarely land in your lap, particularly those that are most suited to you. Putting yourself in scenarios where those opportunities are more likely to arise is vital.

"[Throughout my career,] I've been listening and learning an awful lot and trying to jump around different areas of different businesses, as well as trying to go alone and work for myself. It's all about consuming as much knowledge as possible to use in the future. If you want to do the same thing forever, you'll only ever think about that realm or that little silo." Matthew.

For Matthew, flow comes through consistently learning and delving deeper into his field. He does this by exploring different roles, areas of the business, and thinking outside of his current role responsibilities. How could you find your flow and develop your skills in areas you enjoy most?

Learning comes in all shapes and sizes.

For many, the idea of retraining, especially if the training is very involved and expensive, can seem impossible, but there may be ways to make it happen.

Learning opportunities are everywhere. They can come from formal learning platforms or institutions, such as universities, colleges, training sites, online videos, mentors or coaches, lectures, seminars, or academic classes. The internet has given us the ability to access training and development courses from all over the world – many of them free – from experts and newbies alike. Sites like Lynda.com, Udemy, etc., offer cheap courses for a range of different skills.

Learning may also come from less formal opportunities, such as talking to friends, colleagues, or family or reading books. These less formal outlets are often free and easy to access. Even many of the more formal outlets are often inexpensive if you spend time researching where to find them.

An artist, Virginia, who is now making a living with her craft, was self-trained. She loves what she does, so she spends her free time watching free or low-priced videos and classes online from other artists. However, if you want to retrain in something that requires formal qualifications, there may be opportunities for scholarships. It's not always easy to afford-ably learn a new craft or find the resources you need, but if something truly interests you, your drive to find those resources will be less likely to wane. That's why it's so important to find the activities that bring you flow. Finding such opportunities requires willingness to put in the work and achieve the goals necessary to make your dreams reality.

Another reason for learning new skills is that it diminishes the risk of being out of work if your role becomes redundant or if you are laid off. You will be giving yourself a chance to move into other areas you enjoy because you already have a foot in the door by understanding different fields, tasks, or roles.

No one knows anything until they learn.

It can feel hard to be new at something. Being new means you're destined to fail until you develop mastery in your chosen subject. Here are some things to consider to support you to feel less nervous as a newbie:

- Don't be afraid to take jobs that aren't necessarily what you see yourself doing longer term while you train yourself in or explore the work you want to do.

- Know that *any* job can help you learn more about what you want and what you don't want.

- Don't be afraid to plunge in at the deep end and try new things. In fact, seek out opportunities to get out of your comfort zone.

- Remember, everyone knows nothing when they start something new.

Even though learning something new can feel daunting, it can also inspire your drive to learn more. All you have to do is begin.

"If I've been out of learning for a while and not studying, I can feel less stimulated. Instead, I try to go to meetings or seminars to continue professional development, I keep reading, and I stay interested in [new psychological] theories. I think this is what keeps me feeling driven." Yasmin.

You can always learn in your current role too. Even in situations where you might not feel engaged, there can be opportunities to learn if you truly listen to the people around you.

"I don't say anything for quite a long time [in meetings]. I just listen, because if I'm saying something, then I'm not learning anything. Generally, if I don't know anything about the topic, I am happy for people to talk at me, and I'll just try to gain some insight. The best thing is just to listen. That way, you can learn." Matthew.

This active listening may present opportunities to join people on new projects, support people who are struggling with things that either interest you or you have skills in. It may also help you develop an interest in something new.

"I'm lucky in the respect that every time I have done a project with somebody, I have learned something from it, and then I think I could offer it as a service [in my freelance work]." Emily.

On-the-job training, rather than the formal marketing course she studied, is what helped Emily transition out of bar work and into a career she wanted.

"A woman, called Cassie, who had just set up her own distribution company, was [working alone as] a

one-woman band and desperately needed somebody with contacts in the drinks industry who could do sales on a door-to-door basis and could also provide marketing support. She basically needed a jack of all trades, and I was really keen to learn from somebody who had such an entrepreneurial spirit and was already highly lauded for her previous career. She'd worked on a brand that had got her lots of accolades and had made her like almost like a household name in the [hospitality] industry. [I got to work with] a company that was really at a grassroots level until it became a seven-figure business. The marketing course helped, but really, the work itself was my training." Emily.

However, sometimes more formal courses can be the catalyst into a career that inspires you:

"I did a short 10-week course in psychotherapy, which was only £200. At the time, I thought I could do only the first five weeks and then not continue [if I didn't enjoy it]. It sounded really affordable. I did the course, and it changed my life. I realized this was where I needed to be; I loved it. It was so stimulating. So interesting." Yasmin.

"When I was looking at doing some new career coaching qualifications with Henley, one of my mentors said to me, 'You've been doing this for years. Why do you

want to do another course? Do you need to?' I spoke to a couple of other people who'd actually done a course, [who said the course was invaluable]. [I thought,] you can teach an old dog new tricks! It helps you refresh, you know? If I look back at my last formal training, which was 19 or 20 years ago, things have changed; there are new models and new ways of thinking." Richard.

Never give up on what you want.

Now may not be the right time to work on what you love, but that shouldn't stop you delving into subjects you enjoy.

A friend of mine, who is a CMO at a financial firm, played to her strengths by crafting a career in marketing because she had an interest in it in her youth and she showed an aptitude for it. She still enjoys the field and her work, but she often tells me that she feels she missed out. She really wanted to go into finance, but she came straight out of college with grades that meant she couldn't follow a formal financial training path. She fell into a job as a marketing assistant at a local company. Once she began to appreciate the money she earned, she felt she could never take time out from work to study her real passion. She believes if she'd had a more supportive schooling environment and some encouragement from home to hone her interests, she would have studied her passion.

This woman played to her strengths and works in an area she's good at, but she doesn't work in an area she loves. She spends a lot of time outside of work working on her passion. She reads numerous books and papers and watches videos and tutorials to learn about financial models. She has become extremely knowledgeable. Eventually, she hopes to work in the finance field, but she needs to put her family in a financially secure position first. These dual goals keep her motivated, and she tries to apply what she learns at home to her job and the company she works in until she can follow her own dream and do more of what she loves.

While doing what you love is, naturally, the best way to love what you do, doing what you're good at to generate an income and then focusing on what you're passionate about on the side can still help you have a happy work life, especially if you look for ways to incorporate what you love into what you do day-to-day.

The key to continuing to feel happiness in your work – whether that's paid work or working on activities that bring you joy outside of work – is to keep working on the things that bring you happiness in your life. When you never give up on ways to bring more of those joyful activities into your work, you will constantly feel the benefits of living a life that brings you passion and contentment.

CHAPTER 8

FINDING FEEDBACK FROM MANY SOURCES

For people who love to work, there is often a need for feedback. But not always the kind of feedback you might expect in the way you might expect to receive it.

Some people like feedback directly from others. They seek face-to-face recognition for the work they do, and they know that receiving feedback in this way makes them thrive, so they look for ways to get it. Some get feedback by recognizing changes in their environment; they see that they have improved something around them. Perhaps their client's skill at a task has improved through their teaching program, or someone's understanding of themselves has developed through therapy. Others get feedback from their customers, seeing if they are happy with their ideas or work. Some can also get feedback from themselves. They ask themselves throughout a project or task, or when they have completed a piece of work, what they enjoyed or didn't enjoy about that work. They spend time reflecting on the task through journaling or sharing their thoughts with a coach or mentor.

When you love what you do, feedback can be personal.

People who love what they do invest more of themselves into their jobs. From the numerous interviews I had with people who love to work, I found that, when I asked them to describe what a 'bad day' looked like for them, they told me it was when someone cancelled a project in which they had invested their time and effort.

> *"There was a project that I'd worked quite hard on. In my opinion, we'd developed a good pitch, but [we didn't get the project]. I took that quite hard, but only because I'd thrown a lot into it."* Stuart.

Another example of someone who is heavily invested in her work is Emily, a freelancer and parent, whose partner works away from home frequently. She shared a story with me about a day when both herself and her two children had stomach bugs and she had to deliver a project, or risk not getting paid, between vomiting. She felt a responsibility to the project and her client, and she knew delivering the project on time was important to her. Receiving the feedback that she had done the best for her client was so important to her that she delivered on her promise despite being so ill.

Because these people are personally invested in the work they do, losing or failing at a project is personal to them. It's not just 'work'; it's an important part of their lives and they want to give their best. When you love your work, you want to know that you are having a positive impact, so feedback regarding the time invested is a vital part of moving your mission forward. You want to know you've done a good job, and if you haven't met the mark, the impact personally affects you.

> *"I don't like it when I have built a very strong story [about the best design for a product or series of products], the business case is absolutely spot on, and there isn't a reason why we shouldn't do something, but it doesn't happen. It just feels like a waste of time. You've got all the facts to back it up [the viability and feasibility of a design approach] but it doesn't get the sponsorship. But from a design point of view, some lecturers always told me that you've got to be willing to burn your babies!"* Matthew.

Choose feedback wisely.

Career Agents don't always take on others' feedback; they only use it when they consider it to be valuable. When you love your work, you are more inclined to trust yourself enough to a) know when you are onto a good thing and b) believe that sometimes you need to make your own mistakes without following advice from others.

"The funny thing is, regardless of what my mentors and managers and people that I really respect have said, I've got on with what I wanted to. I own my mistakes and successes, but I have always been quite open about getting advice, because I want to have a balanced decision-making process. I make my own decisions, but I get feedback from a series of individuals who may not necessarily agree with me." Sophie.

Ultimately, when you love what you do, you chart your own path. You listen to others and use feedback when it will take you where you want to go, but you make your own mistakes and keep moving forward on your own journey.

Sometimes, this helps you push ahead, but one of the most important things I learned about people who love what they do is the depth of self-awareness they have. Even when they recognize that they might chart their own path and do things their way, they know when to look for help and support because they understand where their weaknesses lie and where extra guidance might be useful.

"I can be quite focused, but not all the time. I can be quite blinkered, and I'll just bulldoze ahead with things. I really need people to recognize that in me and know why I'm doing it but also be able to reign me in a bit, put me back on the right track, give me guidance, and make me think about things I hadn't considered." Elizabeth.

Trusting your own feedback.

I recently began a daily writing practice, which I found in a book by Julia Cameron called *The Artist's Way*. In the book, the author suggests the importance of writing 'morning pages'. These are three pages of 'stream of consciousness' writing, aimed at giving you time in your day to focus on what you're thinking and feeling without judgement. I see these pages as a form of mindfulness; an opportunity to be in the present moment; just me, my pen and paper, and my thoughts.

By doing this kind of practice, you gain increased self-awareness of what makes you happy and sad, what motivates and invigorates you, and what drives you crazy. You learn about yourself. You may think that you already know yourself, but in the past, I've spent a lot of my time going along with what others need from me or want from me without truly stopping to think about what *I* want and need.

By stepping back, you can begin to learn about how you want to interact with the world. You discover your habits and how to break them and work on new ways of interacting that help you thrive.

Self-reflection doesn't have to come through writing; it can be as simple as asking yourself questions or stopping to consider what may or may not work for you and why.

"Through my network, I've recently been having conversations with people who say, 'we think you'd be great for this [contract role]. I'll say, 'Why do you

think that role [would suit me?]', and they'll say, 'I worked with you on 'x, y, z' and you're really good at it, and I saw that it is something you'd really enjoy.' I might listen and say, 'I know why you think I'd be good at that, but that isn't what I actually enjoy. So, where you're thinking about directing me is not actually what I want to do." Maurice.

Self-reflection on feedback and insight is key. Asking yourself, 'what do I think?' is something we often overlook, preferring to get feedback from others. But when you start to trust your own feedback, it can be a very valuable indication of what is going well and not so well for you.

"Whenever I deliver a project, I sit back and ask myself, 'What was it about this project that I enjoyed? Was it the location? Was it the people? Was it the interactions?' and 'Where can I find these things in other roles?" Maurice.

Feedback can also be found when you stop doing something and realize it was draining you. I recently spoke to a friend of mine who works for herself as a marketer. She was trying to build her client portfolio and had a goal of four clients. While completing the work for her existing three clients, she continued cold emailing potential new clients to find her fourth. One day, one of her clients came to her and said he couldn't afford to keep her on. She was concerned because this client was a fundamental part of her income, but she was secretly relieved because of the amount of time she'd been putting into his work. She didn't enjoy the work she did for him, but she felt she couldn't walk away from it because she needed the income.

Once she stopped working for him, she found that she had more headspace and could finally think more clearly about what she wanted and where she wanted to take her business. Because of this, she was able to take some time to be mindful about her options. For a couple of days, she spent a lot of time 'staring into space', as she put it. She hadn't realized just how much this work had been draining her mental resources. She was able to regroup and find the creativity in her brain again.

If she'd stopped to ask herself how things were going for her and spent time considering her other options rather than using every spare moment to 'do the work', she might have moved away from the draining work sooner. Continual self-reflection is a vital part of loving what you do.

Feedback and accomplishment.

Feedback from something you've created becomes valuable when you've invested your energy into making that thing the best you can. The project becomes a personal investment of your time and resources, so when it works out and you see the fruits of your labor, you feel satisfied.

You know you had to learn some skills in depth to be able to deliver that project effectively and see it work. The outcome of that project is a form of feedback.

"When it's something that you've developed and it's turning a profit, that's a great feeling [of accomplishment]. On a personal level, it's great going into someone's house and seeing something, [such as a kitchen], I've designed." Matthew

"IT transformation has really been my career for the last 25 plus years. It involves hands-on delivering process improvement, seeing success and walking away thinking, 'actually, we've moved someone forward with that intervention, which wouldn't have happened otherwise'. That's what gives me a kick." Maurice.

Even when the feedback isn't immediate, the feeling of achievement is still a powerful form of feedback.

"It's different to being 'on the tools', [building in person rather than being the architect or designer], but in a design capacity or manager capacity, you're still doing something that you put on paper, whether [or not] it's a few years down the line. So, there's that element of feeling satisfied when you've done something worthwhile." Stuart.

"I really like seeing the impact that [therapy] sessions can have or when clients come back in, reflecting on something that we've spoken about. I can see something opening up in their lives that we've explored or talked about, and I love seeing that long term effect." Yasmin.

"I get validation from people who work with me and come back to work with me again and again and again." Emily.

Feedback is an invaluable resource for growth.

Sometimes you see yourself one way and everyone else sees you in another. 360-degree feedback is an approach that collects feedback from many of the people you work with in different capacities. Managers and colleagues provide feedback about their perceptions of your strengths and weaknesses. Sometimes their perceptions can surprise you.

"Early in my career, I thought I was really good at thinking up new ideas and driving them forward. Then I got feedback which basically said that I wasn't good at my job at all! [The feedback said] I take other people's ideas, formulate them into a process or structure and get [the project] done. I was gutted! I thought I was the guy everyone went to for ideas!

Now, I've realized I'm the guy in the room who gets the bright ideas out of the bright people." Maurice.

People who love to work display integrity in their work. They don't just want to 'win' and get positive feedback at all costs; they want to deliver something that's useful for whoever they are delivering it to; but something that also showcases their skills.

"If I say the wrong thing [in a sales presentation], there's always a possibility that I can lose the deal. If I win or lose the deal, it has a financial consequence. But [the deal] has to be a win for them [too], [because that's important to my integrity as a salesman.] If [the deal] is not the right solution, I don't want to push it. When I look at my successes, it's those deals, [the deals where my company, the client, and I won], that I can look back on and be proud of." Denny.

The small things matter because you're personally invested in the outcome.

Sometimes, we crave positive feedback; feedback that tells us we've done well or that we're achieving. We want this type of feedback because it makes us feel good. Actually, it's the constructive feedback that helps us grow and learn, and when you love what you do, even when the developmental feedback may sting a bit, you seek it out because you know it will help you improve in your chosen field.

> *"I spend a lot of time inside, painting and not talking with anyone, but when I finally post my work on Facebook or Instagram and I start receiving feedback, it's amazing, because I suddenly get a lot of interaction with people around the world. I receive thousands of encouraging messages, but if just one person tells me that they don't like something, I have to fix it."*
> Virginia.

Other times, the feedback isn't always forthcoming or easy to find; you have to look carefully to find subtle changes in behavior. However, these small changes, those that help you go from good to brilliant at your craft, are the most fulfilling.

> *"I think [being a psychotherapist] is the kind of job in which you don't always get feedback. You can't always get amazing feedback from someone, if any feedback at all. Sometimes, the work can feel really rewarding, just seeing subtle kind of differences [in behavior]."*
> Yasmin.

Feedback is vital when you love your work.

My postgraduate psychology study focused on the concept of feedback. Positive feedback is universally well received. Who doesn't like to hear when they've done a good job? Negative feedback, on the other hand, is less desirable to most. A time when people are most open to negative feedback is when they seek it out for themselves. My research showed me that when you actively seek feedback from others, you are more likely to act upon it.

However, the feeling of putting yourself in a vulnerable position in which you don't know whether you will receive negative or constructive feedback can be scary, even if your decision may be to ignore it. That's why loving what you do is an important part of your capability to grow. The sheer joy of getting better at something you enjoy is more valuable than the feeling of despair you might feel due to failing at something. The act of seeking out feedback gives you even more conviction to move forward. The process is a circle of power that keeps you craving more.

It's not all about external feedback. Loving your work is about enjoying the process.

Experiencing psychological flow, or the feeling of being 'in the zone', while doing an activity is a form of feedback. The feedback comes through the feeling that you're able to achieve the task while also feeling challenged by it. The task itself is giving you feedback by saying, 'you can do this', and each increment of the task propels you further on the journey to wanting to do more. You feel capable, so you want to continue.

During flow, you're not aware of time. You're not thinking about what comes before or after the activity; you're solely in that moment. It's not that your deadlines suddenly disappear, it's only that you forget about them for short periods of time and the only thing that feels important is the activity itself.

You lose the feeling of 'being in the zone' when the task or activity becomes too challenging or when you don't feel you have the sufficient skills to complete it. The reason why one activity brings you flow when another might not come down to whether you're completing the activity for an external reward, such as money or a gift. When you're truly experiencing psychological flow, you're absorbed in the moment of the activity because you enjoy it for its own sake.

What if you can't find feedback?

Finding feedback isn't always easy. Perhaps you're yet to find flow-producing activities so you're not gaining useful positive feedback or reinforcement from tasks you're doing. Perhaps the people in your company, managers, colleagues, or people you manage, aren't giving you feedback on your work. Perhaps you work remotely from home or another location, so you barely see your team. Or perhaps you work alone.

If this is the case, here are some ways you can find feedback:

- Give feedback to those around you. When you set the example, others may feel more inclined to share feedback with you.

- Ask for feedback. Even when people don't readily give feedback, when you ask for it, they may feel more inclined to share it.

- Look for ways in which the work you've done is being used by others. Have you designed something that others are using? How are they using it? Sometimes, when something works well, we're less inclined to shout about it than if it has issues. Look for the positive ways in which your work is being used and find ways to implement these ideas elsewhere.

- Explore activities that might bring you psychological flow. Look for things that interest you but that also challenge you enough that you feel you're developing skills but not feeling too challenged that you want to give in.

- Ask yourself for feedback. Remember, *your* feedback is as valuable as anyone else's and asking yourself these deeper questions about an activity can help you shape your career into one that you love.

o What did you enjoy about the task you just completed?

o If you had to complete that activity again, how would you feel? (If this answer is negative, that's a sign that it's time to consider recrafting the task or exploring other ways to use your skills. More to come on recrafting in Chapter 11.)

o How could you complete this task differently to make it more enjoyable?

Without feedback, you may find that you are missing out on progressing faster, even if, at first, you don't recognize that you're missing out:

"I didn't know how to ask for help. I didn't know the whole process [of asking for help or who to ask] when I started, so it took me forever to get through anything." Maria.

When you think about feedback, you may only think of the obvious ways to receive it – from other people – but the tasks you complete, the impact you have on others, and the way *you* feel about an activity are valuable sources of feedback, too.

Feedback from anyone or anything, whether you choose to act on it or not, is a fantastic way to learn, develop, and build a career you love.

CHAPTER 9
BUILDING A CLAN OF INSPIRATION AND RESPECT

I once heard a story about a colleague called Laura. Laura worked in a HR department of a company. She'd just finished her master's degree and was in the throes of her first job after deciding to change career. She had some work experience but little confidence in her new field, despite spending months there while writing her dissertation. The issue with the job was her manager.

Laura used to sit at a desk with her back to her manager, but her manager could still see Laura's screen. The floor wasn't exactly noisy, but there was enough of a background hum for Laura to be unaware when her manager was approaching. She would creep up behind Laura, look at what she was working on, and often tell her it was wrong in some way.

When Laura had to go to her manager's desk to ask her questions or check some of her work, her manager would chastise her in front of her colleagues. Her colleagues took to calling the manager 'The Dragon' and always asked Laura if she was okay after every interaction. With the other staff, the manager was friendly and jovial. Sometimes, she was friendly with Laura, too, but she had a controlling side that she liked to unleash on her only subordinate: Laura.

Laura told me that when she spoke to her manager, she found herself crouching down at her desk; partly to try to prevent people from hearing the manager loudly correcting her work and partly because she felt so intimidated in her presence. Laura told me that she physically shrunk her body to protect herself from her manager's attacks.

One day, Laura's manager was late for work, and, around lunch time, Laura got a phone call from her. She'd had an accident, and Laura would need to take over managing much of her work for the next few weeks. Laura wanted to screech with delight! Not only did she not have 'The Dragon' to contend with any longer, she also had an opportunity to shine.

Many people feel they must suffer bad managers and feel there is no escape. It's particularly difficult when you work in a junior position because you often feel there's a hierarchy to your workplace and that the way people in positions of power treat you is exactly how you *should* be treated.

Laura told me that, now that she's in a more senior position, she wishes she'd realized that nobody has the right to make you feel small or inadequate. There are always opportunities to learn and grow, particularly if you're at the beginning of your career, but those lessons should be learned in a safe environment, not with someone who bullies you.

This story leads us to the final factor that drives people to love their work: Building a clan of inspiration and respect.

The power of people.

Finding the right people to support you in your career can be the difference between success and a constant struggle or source of unhappiness.

One of my interviewees, Stuart, had big aspirations in his childhood for his future career, but the lack of supportive people around him led him off track.

> *"As a child, I had two desires for a career. One of them was to be a policeman, and my second was to work in the space industry, somewhere like NASA. I even made contact with people at NASA and asked for the best way to get a job there. I think the reason why I didn't pursue that was primarily because I didn't enjoy school. It wasn't necessarily because I was bad at learning but because I experienced a high level of bullying."* Stuart.

Stuart's story illustrates the impact that a negative relationship with the people around you can have on fulfilling your education or career aspirations. I'm sure all of you reading this have stories of teachers or managers who have had either a very positive or negative impact on your schooling or career.

I bet many of you have also heard the phrase, 'people don't leave jobs, they leave managers.'

I don't fully agree with this statement because the people around you are only one part of creating a career you love, but if you don't surround yourself with people who support, nurture, and inspire you, even if you love the actual work you're doing, you will soon feel unhappy in your job.

However, if the only thing you like about your work is the people you work with, you still have to do the work, and the dynamic you've created at work could change at any moment. When it's the work that drives you, you'll find yourself naturally building a positive network of people. You know they will help you achieve your work goals and, because what they're doing is likely to inspire you, you may want to help them achieve their goals, too.

Building your village.

The saying goes: 'raising a child takes a village'. As a mum of two young children, I can say that this is wholeheartedly true. We live abroad from where we grew up, so much of our family and friends aren't close by, but, between my husband and I, we've built a network of friends and connections around us that supports us to raise our children. Without our network, life would be exceedingly difficult. But why is that relevant to building a career that you love?

My research showed me that people who enjoy what they do are aware of their needs, their flaws, and their strengths. If there is something they are not good at or something they are struggling with, they find people to help fill that gap.

However, the best people to help you develop in the career that most drives you aren't necessarily the people you would choose to spend time with outside of work.

Having friends at work is important, but it's only one piece of the puzzle. If the only part of your work that fulfills you is the people around you, you will be unlikely to create a career you love. Sometimes, you need to leave behind where you feel most comfortable to take your learning further to have more opportunity to grow in your work.

"I loved working as part of a team. We had a really lovely team whilst I was working there, and I just enjoyed being part of something. The reason why I left that job was because I felt I couldn't be the best organizational psychology consultant I could be unless I had worked in an organization that hires psychology consultants like me to support their business agendas, unless I'd been on the other side. So, I made an active move to find a role within an organization." Nadia.

However, when you find or create a career you love and *then* meet people who share your dreams, aspirations, and goals, or people who challenge you to grow and develop in your work, that's when you get the best of both worlds.

"We sat next to each other for years, and we worked so well together because we're so similar. We had a good crack with each other all the time, which made work so much better. It's great to meet someone who just gets you and who has a similar sort of mindset to yourself." Matthew.

However, the people who inspire you or make your days more fruitful and engaging might not be the people you sit or work next to; they may be people you've never even met.

"I used to watch artists online and think that they seem very natural. I always thought I wanted to paint like them, but I also wanted my own style." Virginia.

You could even find an entire online community.

"I was looking around for a job, and everyone I knew kept saying it's about the people you know. But I didn't know anyone who codes. I'd been doing Free Code Camp by myself. It was then that I realized I had to get on social media." Maria.

Your village of inspiration and respect might sit outside your workplace, or even outside your field of work. Inspiration, support, and a challenge to grow in our careers can come from anywhere if we look for it.

"One of the biggest influences on me was really my mom. From a young age, she really pushed the idea

of leadership and development into my head. I wrote a speech in sixth grade about the power of positive thinking. What I saw in her was a can-do attitude, which was inspirational. I felt I could take on anything and be successful as long as I put my mind to it and had a positive outlook on things." Denny.

Even if you're unsure of the next step in your career, or you haven't yet found ways to bring love into your work, follow the crumbs of your curiosity. Sometimes we believe that the things we think and feel about somethings in life are the same for everyone, and when we feel that way it can be difficult to distinguish what interests, ideas, and sources of inspiration are unique to you. Spend time using the quizzes in this book, and other resources that appeal to you, to learn about yourself and how to follow the things that make you curious. Look for people who stand out to you and try to understand why they stand out. If you haven't got a network around you, go out and find it. I provide ideas for how you can do this later in this chapter and in Chapter 11. If you show willing to learn and move forward, there will always be people out there who will help you on your path.

"Every time I had the fortune of meeting with some-one who took the time to talk to me, I would ask for their recommendations for three other people I should talk to." Lia.

Creating your village is a vital part of building your confidence and opportunities, but if your current scenario is less than positive, take solace in knowing that even difficult scenarios can teach you important lessons. Many people experience scenarios in which they feel they are learning, but while they are going through it, they are miserable:

"My manager didn't care about my feelings, but at the same time, he understood that he had to [support my flexible needs to be there for my children when they were sick], legally! It made me dread him questioning me or [any work I produced], so I always had to second guess what he was going to ask and always be very prepared." Matthew.

"You learn as much from working with bad leaders as you learn from working with great leaders, so the negative moments aren't wasted experiences." Richard.

The important thing to remember when work is challenging, as Matthew describes above, is that, ultimately, you have control over the situation. If someone is making your working life miserable, it's up to you to decide when that misery is a learning opportunity and when you've had enough and it's time to cut ties and move on. That may not necessitate moving on immediately, because such a decision may not be financially viable, but making the decision to explore other options for work is entirely within your locus of control.

What is locus of control?

Your 'locus of control' is a psychological aspect of personality which explains how much you believe you have control over the events that influence your life. A more internal locus of control means that you believe your behaviors control the events that happen to you. An external locus of control means that you believe the outcome of scenarios is more influenced by external factors, such as a difficult boss, the traffic making you late for work, or the challenging computing system you have to work with every day.

Activity

Throughout the coming week, take time to ask yourself the following questions every time you feel that a challenge or negative events you're experiencing are the result of external factors:

1. What three things could you have done to change the outcome of the event?

2. If you had done any one or all of the three things you listed above, what do you think the outcome might have been?

3. How would you feel if you got the predicted outcome rather than the actual outcome?

The exercise above will help you to see the impact of having more of an internal locus of control. It's impossible for every outcome in your life to be influenced by your behaviors; there will always be external factors that create events you cannot change. However, you may find that you have more control over your day than you first thought.

Finding mentors.

In his book, *Sapiens*, Yuval Noah Harari discusses how humans came to dominate the earth. He discusses how, when sapiens (his definition for humans) first came to earth about 2.5 million years ago, we had competition. There were other species similar to ours, but homo sapiens won out in the evolutionary war. His reasoning behind why we won out was because we have an ability to create fictional stories. These stories allow us to collaborate with people from many walks of life and help us work with countless numbers of strangers in very flexible ways. This ability to collaborate allows us to create huge networks of people who can support us when we need them most.

"If I see somebody who drives or inspires me, I want them to be my mentor, and I kind of latch on to them. I currently have a mentor who I can be completely open with. There's no judgment, and she's very open as well, so I feel like there's mutual respect." Elizabeth.

When interviewing people about why they love to work, I found that role models come in all shapes and sizes. A couple of my interviewees have found mentors in the most unlikely places, from TV personalities to Instagram influencers, from revolutionary leaders to next door neighbors. A role model is merely someone you look up to who has mapped a path to the version of success that appeals to you. They might be your neighbor who works as a nanny looking after children in your neighborhood or a film star. A role model is someone who you aspire to be like because you admire what they do and how it has impacted their life.

> *"Wanting to be a builder probably comes from my dad, to be honest, but in my mind, what I wanted to do was borne very early in my life. I loved building things out of Lego, making little cars and stuff from matchbox toys. I'm pretty sure my love for building comes from just playing with this stuff and going into my own little world, probably because I was on my own most of the time, living in a village with not many friends around. It was cast in my mind quite early on that this was what I wanted to do."* Matthew.

One of the people I interviewed talked about a TV show she had watched as a child in the UK. The main character of that show was a forensic psychologist. The way the character interacted with people to help solve crimes had a huge impact on her, and she decided then that this was what she wanted to do for a career when she grew up. She made it as far as studying for a psychology degree and learning more about the role of a forensic psychologist before she found out that what she'd seen on TV was actually far from the reality of being a forensic psychologist! The true role didn't appeal to her at all, so she ended up taking a different path. She still found that doing something that allowed her to work with people and better understand what drove people to act in the way they do was appealing to her, it just wasn't in the guise she saw when she was a child.

Mentors may not be there right at the beginning when you're choosing or changing your career, but finding them can be helpful when you're trying to form your career into one you love. Your network could consist of:

- Family members: parents, siblings, aunts, uncles, cousins;

- Close friends;

- Acquaintances;

- Formal coaches or mentors;

- Online communities.

For years, I've worked as a business psychologist, supporting others to give them more fulfilling working lives. I was convinced, given my skillset, that I shouldn't need help to hone my business and my career because that was the kind of support I give to other people. Why should *I* be asking people for help? Shouldn't *I* be able to give that help to myself?

The problem is, it's hard to criticize your own efforts, and it's hard to walk away from things when you've invested your time and energy. However, it's not hard for someone else to do that for you, particularly if that person is impartial. They don't have the same emotional attachment to the issue that you have.

Finding people to support me in my career is the best thing I've ever done to propel me forward and help me better help others. In Daniel Goleman's book, *Social Intelligence*, he mentions the increased enthusiasm of social workers to give more support to people they care for if they feel cared for themselves. The same goes for any of us in our work.

Coaches and mentors.

What's the difference between a coach and a mentor?

A coach is someone who asks you questions to help you uncover answers yourself. A mentor is more like a teacher who imparts knowledge on you that they have learnt on their journey to success.

A mentor may seem like the more useful option because they'll have methods that they can give you to allow you to begin solving an issue or taking action on something immediately. However, your situation is likely to be unique to you, meaning that the solutions that worked for them may not work for you. This is when coaches can be helpful. They are impartial to your situation. Your family members or friends, on the other hand, may be personally affected by the career decisions you make.

A coach seeks to understand your situation and then asks questions to help you figure out problems and find solutions. With a coach, you'll understand the intricacies of your situation, so you will be more likely to find solutions that are a good fit for you and your life.

Mentors and coaches won't necessarily give you the answers to your problems. Why should they? They won't know your life or circumstances in as much detail as you do, and they won't understand what is and isn't possible for you. However, mentors and coaches can give you new perspectives to think differently about your issues, either by telling you what they did so that you can try it for yourself or by asking you questions that will allow you to dig deeper within yourself to find the answers to your own questions and map your own path. They are also great people to consult to help you push your boundaries. We all have boundaries, even if we don't know it. They help us to think of ways of seeing the world that we may never have thought of. Even if you don't follow a path that they've helped you figure out, you'll have new perspectives on your problems that can help you find other routes to take or other ideas to adopt in the future.

They are also often much better listeners than family and friends! We all need a little push sometimes, and you may just be able to go a little further with your career than you ever believed possible when you get some extra support, encouragement, and inspiration.

CHAPTER 10

HOW PEOPLE WHO LOVE
WORK KEEP LOVING WORK

Now that we've covered *what* people do to build careers they love, we'll explore in more depth the behaviors they use and the psychological factors that influence *how* they approach building careers they love.

To make consistent intentional decisions towards building careers they love, Career Agents follow an array of psychological strategies or behaviors. This chapter aims to highlight some of those behaviors. In Chapter 11, I will go on to explain how you can build such strategies for yourself to build the career you love.

Making choices about what you choose to do and where you work is one thing, but the psychology behind making those decisions or *how* people build those careers is a vital part of what keeps these people loving what they do. As you've read through this book, you may have asked yourself questions such as:

1. What do I do if I can't make the decisions that these people made?

2. What do I do if I feel I'm not good enough at my job to steer my career in the direction I want it to go?

3. What if I don't know what I like to do or how I'd like to do it?

This chapter will help you find the answers to these questions and more.

Few people start off doing what they love.

Not many people wake up one morning knowing the exact career they want, and people rarely 'fall into' what makes them tick. The people who find careers they love try new things and reflect on their endeavors until they find what matters to them, what they're good at and enjoy, and what will give them the income they desire under the conditions they wish to work. Some keep pivoting throughout their lives and careers, so they feel consistently fulfilled in their work.

After reading some of the accounts in this book, you may think many of these people are different to you. Maybe you feel that they always knew what they wanted to do, or maybe you believe they had a little extra help that you don't have.

This may be true in some instances. Some had support gifted to them through family or early childhood experiences, and some found it easy to decide what they wanted to do with their careers to feel fulfilled at work.

However, those who had early support still shaped their careers through their own intentional decisions and steps as they continued to build their roles into something they love, not roles that their parents or peers believed were best for them. Many of the people I spoke to have found their way through trial and error and shaped their careers into roles they love *despite* negative experiences.

Every person mentioned in this book comes from a different background with varying levels of support and a vast array of influences and has experienced many diverse things throughout their lives. They are all unique and yet they share the commonality that they love what they do. The uniqueness of these people and their influences is why I believe we can all love what we do, even if, at certain times in our lives, we have to sacrifice what we love to support the people we love.

If you ever find yourself thinking, 'I'm not sure this is making me happy,' that's when it's time to reflect and search again. It might not be the right time to make changes, but it's time to let yourself know that you're not going to settle for anything less than what you deserve, and what you deserve is to love what you do.

How people keep loving work.

Being someone who loves their work requires you to build your internal psychological resources, which enable you and help you to feel willing to make the right decisions for you.

My research tells me that people who love to work have the following behavioral traits:

1. They believe in themselves

2. They have learned what they're prepared to put up with

3. They push themselves out of their comfort zones

4. They don't lose sight of what they love

5. They've learned (and they play to) their strengths

6. They look after their physical and emotional health

1. They believe in themselves.
Confidence is something I've struggled with for many years, although I've hidden it well. I was always the one to ask questions in high school and university, and I always had an opinion. I guess you could say that I was, and still am, curious about why society operates in the way that it does. But when I got things wrong or when I didn't live up to expectations, I would feel crushed, beat myself up for not being good enough, and worry that people thought I was stupid or inadequate. It was unhealthy and consistently made me question who I am and who I want to be.

However, as the years progressed, I built connections and strategies of my own to deal with my confidence issues. I'm learning to get better at making a show of confidence, which turns into real confidence. I saw similar strategies in many of my interviewees, but some were in their 50s and learned these skills later in their careers. Others were in their early thirties and have been practicing them since their teens.

People who love what they do have confidence in themselves and their abilities to succeed. They are prepared to put themselves out there to get what they want, and they have the confidence to follow their own paths. When they face adversity, they look for ways around the issues while keeping their goals of what they enjoy and where they want to go in life firmly in their minds.

Michelle is one example of someone who charts her own path. She likes to get tasks done quickly and efficiently, and she doesn't allow things to stand in the way! Although initially her approach was met with resistance, once she had the confidence to be herself and do things her way, while also getting effective results, she found that people came to her for help. They appreciated and celebrated her differences:

> *"My old boss used to roll his eyes at me because I was always able to find a quicker way of doing things without always following the processes. [Eventually, he realized] there was always a better, cheaper, quicker way of doing things, and he came to me for help because I took a more practical, pragmatic route."*
> Michelle.

Rather than give in, people who love to work believe in their ability to make changes, and that becomes part of their underlying motivation to work. However, change isn't easy, especially when you're taking on whole industries. To keep doing what you're doing and believe that you can make a difference requires determination and self-efficacy. Career Agents don't give in when the going gets tough; they have tenacity because they care about what they are doing and because their work is important to them. They believe in whatever they are working towards, big or small.

Having a vision for the future can also help you feel confident in your abilities, because that vision guides you to make necessary choices, even if it causes you to run into issues in the short term.

"Even if things do get hard, and maybe at times we don't get to step away or switch off, we still feel motivated because we're working towards something bigger." Nirali.

2. They have learned what they're prepared to put up with.

Matthew loves what he does. His dad is a builder, and Matthew has been building and designing things since he was a child. He told me that he always knew what he wanted to do for work. However, that doesn't mean the industry he's in makes his work easy for him.

He knows he needs to do this job to continue doing the work he loves, but he also believes in his ability to make changes to how the industry works. However, he feels that, to do this, he needs to be accepted into the fold first so he can make subtle changes as he builds trust and influence.

Matthew knows the joinery industry is old fashioned, so he adjusts his behaviors to make his days run more smoothly:

"It's not in my interest not to be liked, so I have to put on various masks to make my day go easier." Matthew

Deciding to take ownership of adjusting your behavior to take your career where you want it to go is a vital step toward loving what you do. Even when something makes you feel uncomfortable, if you've decided to do it anyway, that ownership makes doing the task more palatable. As soon as you feel you've lost control in your career, you'll likely start disliking what you do. Feeling like you have choices to decide when, where, and how you work is one of the foundations of loving your work. When the work situation is bad, once you make the decision to endure it, you can change your mind at any time and start to feel comfortable in the ownership of your decisions. Granted, the landscape may have changed, but even if you'd made a different decision the landscape may still have changed. No-one can predict the future; we can only own what we know at that point in time. One of my mother's favorite sayings is, "no one can make you feel a certain way without your permission."

Remember, you *can* make changes. Whatever scenario you're in, you can change it. Maybe not now, maybe not in the short term, but when you realize what you aren't prepared to withstand, the change is already in motion. The rest is only logistics.

3. They push themselves out of their comfort zones

Going out of one's comfort zones is as challenging for Career Agents as it is for anyone, but people who love their work see the value of pushing themselves. They know that if they don't push themselves, they won't be consistently challenged or be able to grow in the areas they enjoy. Growth is like an adrenaline high; when you fail to keep pushing forward to grow in the areas that interest you, the buzz of what you currently do wears off and you feel stagnant and unhappy. Career Agents keep pushing forward, facing the challenges and setbacks to feel more of the successes and more of the fulfilment in the things they love.

Career Agents know that learning new things is hard. You have to sacrifice time and experience ongoing failure to learn new skills. Those who love their work are prepared to experience that failure over and over to allow themselves to keep developing.

When they make errors in their decision-making, they try another path, knowing that they have learned something on their journey. That doesn't mean they don't feel the pain of loss or failure or feel frustrated that they have to start again, but they don't let it stop them because the gain is greater than any loss they may have experienced when working towards the things that matter to them.

Nadia wasn't only keen to push herself out of her comfort zone and start a business, she also recognized that there are many other women in similar scenarios to her, and she wanted to support them to be able push themselves out of their comfort zones through her work:

> *"I quit my job, and, within a year, I set up Avenir. I couldn't have [set up my business without the support of my partner]. I might have had the ambition, I might have had the desire to do an MBA and set up a business, but unless my partner, who happens to be a man, supports me, I can't do what I want to do. Firstly, my partner has to have the desire to be more active as a parent and secondly, his organization needs to be supportive so he doesn't feel like working less is going to be detrimental to his career. All of those things need to be in place. For me, I was asking, how many other people are in this position? So that was my model after having had a child. There's all this pressure to be the main carer, [but I didn't want that, and I didn't want other people to feel that pressure either].* Nadia.

4. They don't lose sight of what they love.

People who love their work stay true to the areas that inspire them and they remain curious about what else might interest them:

> *"I stayed engaged in my job by pursuing projects that are relevant and rewarding and add value to the business and the stakeholders with whom I work. I also have a number of other responsibilities outside work that I have taken on, which all fit the mold that I've either voluntarily assumed or I've just started doing because I think that it's the right thing to do for the business. And, you know, it hasn't hurt me yet."*
> Matt L.

As owners of Superfoodio, Nirali and her husband, Jag, don't need to be as involved in food preparation as they once were, but the food is what inspired them to start the business in the first place, so they make a point of staying connected to that inspiration:

> *"I know we both enjoy the food side in particular, so we try to get involved as much as possible."* Nirali.

It can be easy to slip into a position of getting a paycheck every couple of weeks or month and giving up your agency to control how your day plays out. Even in junior roles, you still have the power to influence what you do and how you work day-to-day. The vital piece of the puzzle is recognizing that you can make changes, often in subtle ways, to affect your day. You may not see the impact of those changes immediately, but with persistence, you'll be surprised what you can achieve.

5. They've learned (and they play to) their strengths.

When we sign up for a job role, there are often elements of that role that we're good at and appeal to us, but there will be parts that we don't like or that we're not good at. Finding ways to play to your strengths, whether they are in your role or not, is how you shape your career into one you love.

> *"I've had two jobs where I've been in strategy roles. In both settings, my employers shifted my responsibilities to take on more sales and business development. In both those cases, there really wasn't an opportunity to do what I love. So, I continued to spend more of my time on the things that I did love and paid lip service to the things that I was being told to do but didn't really think I had been signed up to do. I eventually reached a point where we had to kind of re-examine what my role was. In one of those situations, I ended up leaving the company to another position outside the organization."* Matt L.

However, it may not be an option just to stop doing part of your role or to stop doing it to the best of your ability. In this scenario, it can be helpful to consider something I discuss more of in Chapter 12: automate, delegate, or relegate.

6. They look after their physical and emotional health.

The activities you do outside work and how they make you feel contribute to the mood states you bring to the workplace. If you're miserable outside work, even if your job is positive, you will likely be bringing negative energy with you when you arrive and feel negative energy as you leave. This energy will affect your work, but it will also impact all other parts of your life.

You need to enjoy the work you do, but as the proverb goes, 'all work and no play makes Jack a dull boy'. For work to have a positive impact on your emotional and physical health, your life outside of work is as vital as your life inside it.

"We definitely found that, when having our own business and being a husband-and-wife team, it's quite hard to stop working because we're both working on the same thing. But there is an element of scheduling time out and deciding 'we're not going to do this at this time, we're going to do something else'. I think you do really have to look after your physical and mental wellbeing as well and make time to go to a gym or do a workout. Make sure to have a breather, as well, so work doesn't take over your life." Nirali.

"I've gone back to thinking about my self-care, like going to the gym and exercising, which I feel I've really neglected over the last five years. I realized how down that got me and how important that is. Now, I prioritize work, going to the gym, working on self-care, and spending time with family and friends. People need to make a conscious effort to do these things." Yasmin.

PART 3

HOW YOU CAN LOVE YOUR WORK

CHAPTER 11
HOW TO CREATE
A CAREER YOU LOVE

I'm originally from Newcastle Upon Tyne in the North of England, where there is a saying, 'Shy Bairns Get Nowt'. In other words, if you don't put yourself out there and ask for something, you will never get what you want in life. This applies to your life both inside and outside of work. People who make their way in the world don't achieve it on their own; they ask for support, help, and guidance from those around them. They ask for opportunities, and they put themselves in situations that may not feel wholly comfortable to reach the goals they want.

Recently, I read a post by a young lady who was in a junior position on a marketing team. She had been tasked with developing ideas for a campaign and she was to take those ideas to her manager for them to present at a management team meeting. She was highly engaged in creating the ideas. She was passionate about the work and wanted to grow and learn. However, she was never invited to the meetings. She kept going to her manager with the ideas and kept hoping her manager would eventually invite her to the meetings. She never did.

The young lady was frustrated at the lack of consideration from her manager but felt she couldn't speak up about her frustrations because she was in a junior role.

As you can imagine, by this point, she was upset at her situation, and her dissatisfaction and helplessness had taken center stage. She had failed to realize that, to get what she wanted, all she simply needed to do was ask. She didn't need to go to her manager and complain about her lack of consideration for her staff. The manager was not telepathic. The lady needed to think logically about what she wanted and go out and ask for it.

When she didn't get what she wanted, she could have put together a case as to why it was important for her to be at the meeting and presented this to her manager or other members of her team. If she'd shown the initiative and tried to get her place at the table, she probably would have been more respected and given further opportunities to grow and develop in her career.

But she didn't have the confidence; she didn't feel it was her place to request what she wanted. She felt she needed to wait to be asked.

Sometimes, we get lost in what we think is right without thinking about what could be. I've learned through similar experiences that it's always best to ask for what you want. Shy bairns get nowt.

Building the career you love.

Throughout this book, you've seen many examples of people crafting careers they love by making consistent, intentional choices about things that matter to them in their careers and lives.

People who love to work continually ask themselves if what they are doing for work is meeting their needs financially, passionately, and flexibly. They ensure that their careers give them what they want and need to learn and grow in the direction that fulfills them and whether they have the right people around them, who respect and lift them to achieve their career goals.

Career Agents don't let anyone else make their career choices for them; they chart their own paths. Some go wildly off the traditional working path; others stick closely to traditional jobs but shape their roles in ways that meet the needs of their employer while also meeting their personal career goals. You can do the same.

Mapping a career you love requires you to understand yourself and your needs and asks you to look back on your life to see what you need to do to take you where you want to go, while enjoying the ride in the process. The destination isn't the best part; for people who love what they do, the journey is the main event.

How you got to disliking what you do.

Throughout childhood, the way you shape your learning is often somewhat limited. Your school curriculum is likely well defined, you're often directed by your parents or caregivers as to which extracurricular activities you'll do, and the focus will often be on building a career that is sustainable and provides an income that will allow you to support yourself into adulthood. My experience from working as an organizational psychology consultant tells me that as you transition from education into your working life, and as your experience builds, you are one of the lucky ones if you have conversations about what will give you a fulfilling career and help you build a life you love. When we think about work, passion usually comes second; income is the priority.

You may be lucky and have had a parent or teacher that helped you shape a career path that brings you joy, meets your future economic needs, makes you feel excited about work, and gives you the social factors you require. Unfortunately, many of us must work these things out for ourselves.

Even when you join the workforce, there are often defined routes that you must follow based on the career you're in. You're often assigned a manager; you don't get to choose who you work for. You have a role description that you must adhere to; you rarely get to decide which projects you work on or how to execute your work. You're often given a set of tools and told that 'this is how we do things around here'.

Effectively, throughout our schooling and working lives, we're conditioned to work in ways that others create for us. These structures make up our carefully managed society and help us achieve many goals, including climbing career ladders, buying or renting homes, and providing for our families.

However, as a result, it's not uncommon to hear about people who have achieved financial or status success only to realize they are miserable. This realization can leave people feeling stuck and confused about where to turn next.

Imagine you have followed the defined path of supposed career fulfillment, you have achieved financial success, and you hold a senior position at or near the top of your ladder. But then you realize that it makes you ridiculously unhappy. What do you do?

Losing control to gain control.

When other people have control over your life, it can create feelings of discontent. You only have to think back to the recent Covid-19 pandemic to recognize the uncomfortable feelings that come with giving up control. In psychology, we describe this as 'cognitive dissonance'. Cognitive dissonance is when you believe one approach is the right way to go about something, but you're put in a position where you feel you have to act incongruently with that belief. To justify your actions and to make yourself feel more aligned and in control, you'll tell yourself it's good for you or beneficial to act in a way that is outside of how you believe you should act.

To make yourself feel better about your lack of control, you'll tell yourself that the time away from your hectic schedule is good for you; that it's time for you to slow down and rethink how you approach your work. In reality, many people want to keep going at the pace they always have and get things done.

The feeling of wanting to continue in that life doesn't mean that time slowing down isn't good for us, but it means we struggle to lose the perceived control we have in our lives until we find new ways to control what we do. The same goes for our careers.

Another example might be a weekly team meeting. You dislike the way the meeting is run, and you feel it achieves nothing but sucking up your time. Perhaps you believe the process used to manage the meeting is inefficient, but you tell yourself that the process makes sense because it's the way head office said it should be or you look for ways to justify the approach because you know you have an opportunity for a promotion, so you don't want to rock the boat.

Unfortunately, telling yourself you're on board with something when what you really feel is that it's not working and you want to make changes can lead to long-term dissatisfaction and unhappiness at work.

Frequently pushing issues such as these out of your mind can lead you to separate yourself from work and see it as just a means to an end. The result is that you will disengage and begin to hate your work. Lia describes how she tried to convince herself she was happy when she was actually miserable in her corporate job role:

> *"I taught myself that this is what society told me I should do to 'be successful'. I was not the real version of myself. In college, I did an acting major, which I tell my organizational development clients, and they always laugh. But doing an acting major was the smartest thing for me because it helped me pretend to be interested in what other people are saying; that the meeting was full of really good ideas; that I actually like my co-workers."* Lia.

Holding yourself accountable.

Getting stuck in the never-ending circle of trying to convince yourself that everything is okay is appealing at first. It keeps you in secure employment, and it allows you to save your energy for life outside work. Unfortunately, it eventually weighs you down, and, ultimately, you'll get so stuck that you'll begin to believe that either change is no longer possible, or life can't get any better.

Ultimately, you'll come to the realization that you've placed the accountability for your happiness in the hands of someone else, and they haven't done a good job.

The hardest part is then recognizing that your working life is no one else's problem but yours. No one is tying your hands to the chair in your office. No one has stuck your feet to the floor of the fast-food joint in which you spend your working hours. No one has stapled the headset to your ears, and no-one makes you stand on a freezing cold building site every day, wishing you were working in the Spanish countryside.

You're there because you chose to be there, and only you can choose *not* to be there or make the experience of being there the best it can be.

However, it's easy to write these words and let you know that you have control over how your career plays out; it's much harder to take those decisions and act on them.

To feel free and able to make decisions about your life, you need to feel comfortable and confident within yourself.

Building your psychological toolbox.

It's all well and good me sharing stories about how you can take different path and make different decisions to help you on your way to building the career you love. Unfortunately, it's not so easy in practice. Deciding to do something and having the courage to do it are two very different things.

To support yourself to build a career you love, you need to build your psychological toolbox.

To help you to build your toolbox, I'll be drawing from the field of 'positive psychology'. Positive psychology emphasizes conditions and processes that support people to perform and feel at their best. I saw countless examples of people I interviewed for my research, displaying the principles of positive psychological approaches.

Career Agents are aware of what makes them feel fulfilled at work and how to manage their general wellbeing through the choices they make related to their careers. They know how to make decisions that support their wellbeing at work rather than drain their energy.

A positive psychology model, called the PERMA model, developed by the renowned positive psychology practitioner, Martin Seligman, provides a useful foundation for how Career Agents build psychological strength and resilience related to their careers. Keeping your wellbeing on track can't happen passively. It takes effort, and you must manage that effort. The PERMA model suggests that there are five factors to consider when thinking about improving your own wellbeing.

PERMA stands for:

A. Positive emotions.

B. Engagement.

C. Relationships.

D. Meaning.

E. Accomplishments.

A. Positive Emotions.

The first element of the model suggests that, to feel more fulfilled in your life, generating positive emotions is one of the main factors you must manage. It's impossible to separate your general wellbeing from your wellbeing at work; one naturally influences the other, and you can't 'switch your feelings off' when you step into work anymore than you can switch off what happens to you when you step out of work. Managing your wellbeing to generate positive emotions both inside and outside of work helps you to have a more fulfilling career.

To generate positive emotions within your working life, you can:

1. Surround yourself with people who inspire you, challenge you, support you, encourage you, and pick you up when you're down. Every person I interviewed had carefully surrounded themselves with the right people to take them in the direction they wanted to go.

They did this by self-reflecting enough to understand what they do and don't want in their working life and then found people who could help them on their journey to building this life.

Some of them did this consciously by looking for people who could be mentors or coaches, either in person or through media channels. Others did this somewhat unconsciously by gravitating towards the people who had similar outlooks and views on life to themselves.

Other times, people actively sought out or chose to stay in situations with people who didn't necessarily inspire them in a positive way. They stayed because they felt they were gaining something by putting themselves in difficult circumstances and using what they learned from those challenges to take them forward.

If you're surrounded by people who don't inspire, challenge, support, and encourage you, it may be time to make some changes.

2. Look after your physical wellbeing by exercising regularly and eating food that fuels your body. Many of my interviewees talked about the importance of fueling themselves with healthy lifestyles to feed their minds and bodies. These lifestyles weren't necessarily Instagram-worthy perfect, but they knew they worked for them and gave them energy when it came to how they ate and exercised.

I'm not a nutritionist, so I'm not going to share insights into how to do this; there are plenty of experts in the fitness and nutrition space who can talk with more authority on this subject than I can.

3. Keep your inner demons in check. We all have inner negative self-talk; voices in your head that tell you you're not good enough or you can't achieve something. Career Agents don't have ways to switch off those voices, but they do have ways to manage the demons. You can read more about this in the 'Recognizing your thinking' section in Chapter 12.

B. Engagement.

Have you ever found yourself so engrossed in something that you have forgotten what time it is? Do you get to the end of a workday and wonder where the hours went? You were likely experiencing a phenomenon known as 'psychological flow'. As I've explained earlier in this book, flow theory, created by Mihaly Csikszentmihalyi, suggests that, if you find a sweet spot between having the appropriate skill level you need to complete a task and a level of challenge that pushes you slightly out of your comfort zone, but not so much that you feel you are incapable of achieving the task, you're experiencing 'flow'. Finding flow can bring many positive benefits:

1. You may gain new skills. When you're pushing yourself to the edge of your comfort zone, it may require you to dip your toe into something that you haven't tried before. Because you are 'in the zone', so to speak, you're likely to feel a greater sense of confidence with your ability to achieve at that point in time. This is because you're getting feedback from the task, which is telling you that you're doing a good job. You're not distracted by negative voices in your head saying that you're not doing something right or that you could do better. At this time, your greater sense of confidence may push you to try something new and surprise you at your ability to achieve it and enjoy the new learning.

2. You'll become better at the skills you already have. Since psychological flow arises when you're challenging yourself enough that you're learning something new, but you feel skilled enough in the activity that you feel you can achieve the new task, you're in a scenario in which you're learning and developing yourself. The more you practice and develop your skills at an activity, the better you'll become at executing it.

3. It will make you feel good. Flow generates intrinsic motivation. Intrinsic motivation arises when the task itself gives you a good feeling while you're completing it, rather than you receiving something external to the task, say a financial reward, a sweet treat, or feedback from someone else.

You're also reinforcing that you have mastered something at a particular level, which brings a sense of confidence and self-efficacy and encourages you to want to do and try more new things.

4. You'll feel a sense of control. Finding flow in a task can give you a sense of accomplishment, achievement, control, and wellbeing. You know you're becoming a master at something that you're learning. You know that learning allows you to dig deeper into a subject and explore ideas and insights that others may never have imagined.

C. Relationships.

Having positive relationships in your life helps you build your self-confidence and self-efficacy and gives the feeling that you can achieve whatever you desire. I have talked about the importance of surrounding yourself with the right people, but here I'm going to show you how finding people who inspire you can help you build a more positive and fulfilling working life.

One way to build these feelings in your career is to look for people who have achieved the things you would like to achieve and consider how they did it. These people are much easier to find than ever before. There are online sources everywhere showing people from all manner of different backgrounds living their lives in ways that work for them.

What you might struggle to find is the evidence that most of those people will have struggled and failed many times before they achieved the success of feeling comfortable and happy in their chosen career paths.

The trick here is to find the people who have yet to make it, the people who are at the beginning or middle of their journey, or to work out what the 'successful' people did in the beginning.

The factors that differentiate those who achieve the feeling of being fulfilled in their work are, never giving up working towards what motivates them, and consistently looking for small things along the way that inspire them and make the journey fulfilling. When they inevitably fail, they pick themselves up and give it another shot.

When you surround yourself with other people who are trying, failing, and achieving things you want to achieve, it can make those tasks seem more achievable.

These are the traits to look for and emulate, and these will help you build your belief that you too can build a career you love.

D. Meaning.

Finding meaning in your work and home life means finding something that you're working towards that is larger than yourself. That could be, for example, creating a better life for your child or working towards giving something to a charitable organization. It could also be something like building a business or supporting a colleague to develop their skills. Anything that inspires you or gives you a sense of purpose will help bring meaning to your life.

Don't fall into the trap of thinking that what inspires you needs to be world-changing; it doesn't, it just needs to be enough to change *your* world.

E. Accomplishments.

When you get stuck in a career that doesn't bring you fulfillment, the feeling of wanting to accomplish things becomes less appealing. You may want to achieve tasks so you can get them out of the way and move onto other things, but there's little or no feeling of satisfaction in achieving those tasks, and that's when meaning and positive emotion gets lost.

Learned helplessness is a phenomenon founded by Martin Seligman, which arises when you experience many scenarios of failing to achieve your goals or feeling like the goals that you're achieving don't have any meaning for you. Over time, you feel worn down and no longer want to keep trying. You've learned to be helpless because you don't receive anything positive from being active in your work.

Career Agents have found the things that matter to them, and they continually look for ways to accomplish more in their field of expertise because it gives them a sense of accomplishment and it makes them feel good.

Even when people who love to work are faced with a feeling that they might fail at whatever it is they are trying to achieve, they strive to achieve anyway because the feeling of potential accomplishment drives them to keep going.

"I was listening to a podcast on becoming a mindful leader, and one of the interviewees left their email address at the end of the podcast. I dropped her an email and said, 'I would love to talk to you because what you do sounds amazing.' She replied, and I met her for coffee. I may get rejected sometimes, but I don't take that to heart, as I may well get a response."
Bhavisha.

Changing your behaviors will change your outcomes.

One of the most prominent factors influencing how engaged you feel at work or how positive your experience is at work is the relationships you have with a) your manager and b) your co-workers. Many of you will have heard the term 'people don't leave jobs, they leave managers.' I've even mentioned this same phrase earlier in this book. Well, it's true to some extent. The relationships in your life have a direct influence on your happiness. They are, of course, as I explained earlier, not the only factor that influences your happiness, but they have a large impact, and one you can influence.

To shift the behaviors you experience at work, a good place to start is to look at your own actions. Remember, you can't change the behaviors of others; you can only shift how you act. That doesn't mean you need to put up with negative behavior, but the easiest way to change your environment is to start with working on yourself.

Here are some tools that can be helpful for changing your behaviors:

- If you don't get goals given to you at work, make your own goals. You'll be more likely to strive for them if they are yours. Make sure they're meaningful to you.

- Take free courses in topics that interest you. You never know what you might learn, who you might meet or the opportunities it might open up for you.

- Recognize others and they will begin to recognize you too.

- Model the behaviors you would like to see in others.

- Take your vacation time and take short breaks at work; these will help you to spark more creative thoughts and feel refreshed.

- Know when to let go of something. See when something is failing and make a conscious choice that it's time to move onto the next thing.

- Ask for a 'seat at the table', and if you don't get it, prove that you deserve it. If you still don't get it, find somewhere else that will give you that seat. With that level of persistence, I can guarantee you deserve it.

- Plan your own career path and look for ways to develop it, either in your current organization or elsewhere.

While shifting your behaviors can lead to others acting differently too, sometimes, despite your efforts, nothing changes. If you experience this scenario, you must make a choice. Are you prepared to stay where you are even if it is making you unhappy, or do you need to make changes?

Remember, change doesn't all need to happen right now; making changes in your career is something you can do gradually. You can spend time exploring what you like and dislike about your job first. But remember, it is rare for a person to love everything about their job!

Side note: checking in with your mental health.

If it has got to the point where you feel that everything you do for work (and potentially outside of work, too) is making you miserable, it could be time to seek professional help.

Organizational psychologists, coaches, and perhaps your HR team or manager can help you when your work is making you feel unhappy, but when you feel a general sense of apathy about life, you could be suffering from depression. A trained psychotherapist or mental health psychologist can support you with this scenario. If you feel this way, the first step is to see your doctor.

One thing to note is that whatever your situation, you should never feel you need to accept inappropriate or abusive behavior. If you feel you may be experiencing physical or emotional abuse at home or at work, please seek support from your doctor.

Recognizing burnout.

Burnout is when you experience mental or physical exhaustion because you have been under too much stress for too long.

Learning to recognize the signs of burnout in yourself is one of the most important things you can do to help build and sustain a career you love.

Even if what you do is something positive, brings you joy, helps out others, and gives you a sense of wellbeing, you can still reach burnout. You must make sure you are looking after yourself. If you spend all of your time and energy on helping others, you will eventually deplete your own resources and crash.

To avoid burnout, listen to your mind and body frequently and find ways to assess when you need to make changes. One way to do this is to write down what you feel and the impact that these feelings have on your mood. Consider these questions:

- What brings you joy?

- How much joy are you getting in your life right now?

- What challenges you in a positive way?

- How much time are you investing in those challenges?

- What makes you feel most accomplished?

- How many of these activities are in your life?

- What exercise do you enjoy most? Doing a type of exercise that you hate will not bring you joy, so look for something that makes you feel good about yourself, and you'll be more likely to stick at it.

It doesn't matter what the answers to these questions are; joy might be found in making a meal for your family or working on your PhD. The point is that this joy is yours and it fills you up. Learn what those things are that interest and excite you and aim to fill your life with more of them. This might seem like a simple task, but the act of writing those things down can make them seem more urgent and real and can help you plan ways to bring more of them into your life.

Making choices that meet all your career needs.

When I chose my postgraduate study options, I chose what I loved, what interested me, and what sparked a fire in me. I didn't consider what the career path and financial outcomes of my choices would be. I wish I had, because it's been tough to find my way in this career as there are so many different pathways you can take with a psychology skillset.

I've met many people who've made similar mistakes or people who have done the opposite and chosen study paths that meet the requirements for a financially secure career and not thought about what they want from a fulfillment perspective.

The key to building a career you love is weighing up both options: consider what interests you, but also think about whether you can make an income from it that will meet your needs now and in the future.

You too can love your work.

At school, we're not often taught to self-reflect on what we want from our careers. Discovering what we do and don't like comes through trial and error.

We often take jobs or tasks within our jobs thinking that they will turn out one way, but you end up doing things you weren't expecting or weren't in your job description. Or you do something believing that it's the right path because you're good at it, but quickly realize you hate doing it. We spend a lot of time trying to figure out what we do and don't enjoy and how we can shape our lives to include more of what we love. However, if you spend the focused time working on yourself and understanding what makes you tick, you might find you can achieve loving your work much faster.

Think about the positive impact that something joyous outside of work can have on how you feel that day or at that point in time. Consider an afternoon spent with a good friend, laughing and having fun. That activity can help you feel happy for a few hours, maybe even days.

What if work could give you positive feelings that you could take back into the rest of your life? What if work could be a source of joy, inspiration, and energy in your life, like it is for those mentioned throughout this book? What if you, too, could love your work?

Working in a job that gives you enough income to enjoy life outside of work is a vital part of creating a career that you love, but it's not the only part. You spend a significantly larger amount of your time at work than you do outside of work. Don't waste that time doing something you hate.

CHAPTER 12
TAKING A DIFFERENT PATH: CAREER CHANGE

When I was in my mid-twenties, I was working in the accounts department at a finance firm in London. How I got there was due to a series of bad choices and little guidance from my school. You see, when I was 14, I wanted to be an engineer like my dad, so I chose to study mathematics, physics, and business studies. These choices were perfect for a career in engineering, but not for much else that interested me.

Sadly, after my dad arranged for me to spend a few days on site with civil engineers, - and dressed me in an over-sized yellow rain mac because it poured with rain the entire time - I soon realized that civil engineering wasn't for me. Unfortunately, with the subjects I'd chosen, my degree options were limited. So, I opened a university prospectus, made a list of my options, moved my finger over the list with my eyes closed, and chose a course. That's how I found myself studying computing and statistics.

For the next two years, I gave my bare minimum to that course. I partied hard, made some wonderful friends, and then came down with a mystery illness just as I was starting my placement year in London.

A year into the illness, having had to leave my placement, return home to live with my mum, postpone my course, and spend much of my time in bed, I found out I had chronic fatigue syndrome (CFS).

Two years later, I thankfully recovered. However, during that difficult time, I was determined not to let the grass grow beneath my feet. Having left my partying days behind me (way before I was mentally ready, but seemingly at a time when my body was ready), I became focused on completing my degree and getting my life back. However, this was 20 years ago, and there wasn't the computing infrastructure in place to allow me to access the computing programs I needed from home.

Because I was still clueless about what I wanted to do with my career, I decided that knowledge of accountancy would complement my business studies, so I chose to complete my degree with an elective course in accounting.

My accounting qualification landed me my first job in London, but at age 24, with a degree in computing and accountancy, and a few years of work experience under my belt, I decided I hated numbers. I knew what I'd learned would be useful to me, but it didn't light me up.

I was working in the financial hub of London and surrounded by people managing trading platforms, which involved loads of screens and flashing lights and numbers. But I wasn't interested in what the numbers meant; I only wanted to know how and why the people watching the screens made the decisions to press the buttons. I wanted to understand how they managed the stress of the decision-making with so much information presented to them. It was the psychology behind the trades that drove me, so I then had to figure out how to map a way to working in psychology with qualifications in everything *but* psychology.

I happened to work in an office that was close to the elevator entrance of our floor. All visitors to the floor had to walk past me to get to the rest of the office. We didn't have enough visitors to warrant getting a receptionist, but we had enough that they needed someone to meet and greet passing folk. I volunteered for the job. Now straddling two roles, I had made myself appear versatile and I knew the comings and goings of the office. With these roles in hand, I was then given the role of managing the office supplies. Again, this was a role that needed doing, but not a full position. Over the coming months, when the partners of the firm were looking for someone to support them with their travel booking and diary management, I became the obvious choice.

By the time I left that company, I was an accounts and executive assistant and office manager. I'd opened up doors to allow me to look for roles outside of being an accounts assistant should I so please, and I did.

I went on to become an executive assistant, something which I enjoyed much more, but I soon realized it wasn't what I wanted to do long-term. However, I loved interacting with people more than screens. I knew I needed to delve deeper into my desire to learn more about people, so this was when I decided to begin studying again.

I chose an evening course in psychology. One thing led to another, and three years later, I had an MSc in Occupational (or Organizational) Psychology. I moved from full-time working to part-time working to allow me to study but still have an income. I lived with various friends and family and managed my finances to make it work. I'd also saved some money before I started, which paid for the course.

Now, 13 years later, I'm embedded in my career as an organizational psychologist, and boy am I glad I made the change! It was hard studying throughout my twenties. I sacrificed a lot of nights out with friends, and there were times when I wanted to throw in the towel, but I kept going because, ultimately, the subject interested me.

The subjects I chose at school, and then university, led me to getting stuck in my career, but with some ingenuity, determination, and a lot of hard work, I found a way to my true passions: psychology and writing.

Finding your flow in your career is not always easy, but if you don't allow yourself to settle for something you hate, I'm convinced you can find a path to work that you love.

This is my story and only one of many career-change stories out there. It is also the experience of a young woman without responsibilities or dependents. While I had challenges to face, it didn't matter where I lived or who I lived with because I only had to worry about myself.

However, that doesn't mean that being older and having responsibilities is an excuse to stay stuck in your career. One of my interviewees had four young children and a husband who worked away from home. She homeschooled her kids while transitioning from being a waitress at Olive Garden to retraining to become a full stack developer. She is a constant reminder to me that anything is possible.

Do you really hate your current job?

If the answer is 'yes', I urge you to think more deeply about your answer. I can guarantee that you don't hate everything about it, but if you're at the stage where you feel that you do, then you're going to need to unlearn that thinking before you can make effective steps towards building a career that's right for you.

You might believe you hate your job if:

a) You wake up every day dreading going to work.

b) Your day off is ruined by the thought of work the next day.

c) You're consistently snappy or sarcastic with your co-workers.

d) You make frequent mistakes in your work and with little thought regarding its impact on others.

e) You watch the clock waiting until you can leave.

When you feel you hate everything about your job, it's often because the more challenging things have worn you down so much that they have taken the joy out of the good stuff. Rediscovering the good stuff is your clue to creating a fulfilling career.

The following 'Do you really hate your job?' questionnaire will help you delve deeper into your work and see where you truly need to make changes. Answer each of these questions honestly and in as much depth as you can.

Assessing if you really hate your job.

- What is the first thing that comes into your head when you think about work?

- How do you nourish yourself for the day? What do you eat and drink? Is that food giving you the energy and sustenance you need to get through your day?

- What do you wear to work? How do you feel about your workwear? Even something as trivial as this can help you feel like you have more control over your working day. Taking control in one area can also help you see the possibility of taking control in other areas of your working life.

- How do you feel when you leave for work? What do you like/dislike about heading to work?

- What time do you leave for work? What time do you start? Do you work from home or go to a place of work? How do you feel about these elements of your job?

- Do you commute? What's that like? Does it fill you with joy or dread?

- What happens when you arrive at work? Are you greeted by anyone? Who? How do they greet you? Are there people already there or are you the first to arrive?

- What are your first responsibilities? What feelings do these elements arouse?

- Do you take breaks at work? How do you feel about these?

- Do you have variation in your job, or do you do the same tasks every day? How do you feel about the way your job is structured?

- What do you do for lunch? Do you eat alone or with others? What do you eat and drink? Does this arrangement make you feel fulfilled, unhappy, or indifferent?

- During the day, when do you feel most lethargic?

- During the day, when are you most filled with energy?

- What is your favorite thing about your day?

- What is your least favorite thing about your day?

- What frustrates you most about your job?

- If you have a manager, describe them. When you think about your manager, do you feel positive or negative feelings?

- If you have a team, describe them. When you think about your team, do you feel positive or negative feelings?

- How would you describe the company you work for? Does this description make you feel proud, indifferent, or embarrassed?

- What training opportunities are you offered at work? How do you feel about these opportunities?

- What time do you leave work? Is it easy to leave or do you often get held back? How do you feel about this?

- How do you feel about the financial reward for your work?

- When and from whom do you receive feedback on your work? How do you feel about the feedback you receive?

- If you could work in any industry, what would it be? Why that industry? Is it the industry you're in now? If not, why not? What could you do to get into that industry?

- If you could have any job you like, what would that be and why?

- If you could get paid any amount, how much would that be? Why that amount?

Look back on your answers. Note down which answers you consider positive or negative.

When you have some insight into the more nuanced elements of what you like and dislike about your work, you can begin to see where you'd most like to make changes and what you could keep.

Taking the time to ask yourself these questions gives you the chance to reflect on yourself and will help you make decisions that will more likely meet your needs.

Make decisions wisely; they stay with you.

I read a collection of stories recently (both fiction and non-fiction) by a budding writer who attended Yale University. Tragically, the student, Marina Keegan, died in a car accident the day before she graduated. One of the stories she wrote was about Yale graduates going into jobs in the big four consulting firms because those jobs paid highly and were seen as very prestigious, often only offered to people with Ivy league educations. She wrote about how these students were lured by the status and money and by what society thought they should do having received such highly respected educations. However, many students wanted to pursue other career paths but ended up following the paths laid out for them because they felt they should or had to.

There are many people that fall into the traps of making career decisions that don't reflect what they truly want, and many end up unhappy and unfulfilled. This is a reminder to think wisely about the choices you make; those choices stay with you for life.

Changing career: what it takes.

Changing career (or forging a career that you love) is not for the faint of heart. It takes consideration, careful introspection, time, commitment, and sometimes sacrifice.

When you decide to embark on a specific career path, you're also deciding to leave other paths behind. You're delving into the somewhat unknown. You may have done your research, but you can't possibly know what you haven't yet tried out. This can make forging that path challenging, and this is when it becomes essential to understand your values.

Choose a career that is congruent with your values.

You don't necessarily have to meet all your values through your work, unless you want to. You can meet some of your values with activities outside of work too, but always ensure you're being true to yourself when you decide which values you're prepared to forego when choosing how you work. Ensure you're making choices that will bring you fulfillment day-in-day-out if you want to love what you do.

Knowing yourself and what you need, and continually reminding yourself that you deserve to have those things, will help you build a career and life that matters to you.

How to choose the right job for you.

Know what drives you.

Imagine you have a to-do list in front of you. Who wrote the list? Are you a list-maker?

- How do you work through your to-do list?

- Do you make it to the end?

- Do you do the easy things first?

- Does it take you some time to get started? Do you procrastinate?

- Do you dive right into one task but then get distracted and dive into something else? What distracts you?

- Is your list on a piece of paper? On a smart phone? On your laptop?

- Do you lie awake at night worrying about the unchecked items left on your list?

- Do you wake up at night needing to write down what's on your mind so that you remember to do it the next day?

- Do you have lots of handwritten notes floating about your home or handbag?

I love handwritten notes. They are all over my home, car, and bags. I like to call it 'organized chaos'. It's how I like to work and how I get things done. I know there are better ways to store my to-do lists, but this approach works for me because when things are out of my sight, I forget them. We all have our preferred ways of working, and finding out your preferred methods is the point of this exercise.

These questions may focus on the trivial, such as how you write lists, but they also tell you something about yourself, how you like to work, what annoys you, and what drives you.

Try asking yourself questions like these about various aspects of your life. It will give you some indication of who you might be when it comes to work and will help you better understand what might drive you.

My haphazard notes are an indication of my free spirit. I don't work well if my life is too structured. I need structure to be on my own terms because freedom helps me be creative.

What do your ways of working say about you and how can they help inform you to build a career you love?

To get what you want, you need to *know* what you want.

Choosing a job solely for the salary will satisfy you in the short term, but unless the job brings you deeper intrinsic satisfaction, it will drain you in the long term.

Is your career plan based solely around getting to the next rung on the career ladder? If it is, you may need to be more ambitious.

Imagine your current role:

- Why are you in that role?

- In which industry do you want to be in that role?

- What kind of people do you want to help with your work?

- How much money do you need to live?

- What kind of people do you want to work with?

- Are there other areas of your chosen position or complementary factors that interest you but sit outside your current responsibilities?

- What activities do you like to do outside of work? Can you incorporate these into your current work in any way? Do you want to?

Your role isn't just about doing your job. Your job sits in a wider context. There are likely many people doing similar roles to you from all walks of life, and they all work in different settings. They earn different amounts depending on the areas in which they work, the industry they work in, and the uniqueness of their services.

Thinking about the wider context of your work is a vital part of building a career you love because *why* you do what you do will help you know whether or not you will enjoy *what* you do.

You know more than you realize.

Just because you're in one job doesn't necessarily mean you can't use those skills for another job. It's amazing how easy it can be to rehash your resume to meet the needs of another role. Of course, you should never lie about your skills and experience; not only is this immoral, but it gets you into sticky situations, such as being asked to do tasks that you absolutely do not understand. However, everyone has to learn new things, and the only way we learn is by trying. We all fail sometimes, but we learn by making mistakes and picking up the pieces to try again. Sometimes it can be difficult to persuade someone to give you an opportunity, so you have to think laterally about your skills.

Try searching Google for skills you have and see what appears. This simple act might help you to see the numerous possibilities available to reshape your resume and career path.

An important part of understanding which skills are transferrable is remembering that there is no point in transferring your skills if you don't enjoy doing them.

If you have skill or behavior gaps, it's easy to learn the basics of something through online training courses. There are so many free outlets that you can access to learn all manner of skills. To name only a few:

- ✓ YouTube

- ✓ Udemy

- ✓ Alison

- ✓ Future Learn

- ✓ The Muse

- ✓ Kahn Academy

And there are many more.

When you want change but don't know where to begin.

You've probably read this book because you're considering making some changes in your working life. But not everyone who picks up this book will be at the same stage. Each one of you will be at a different point in your journey.

Knowing the changes you need to make and feeling ready to make those changes are two very different things. By recognizing where you are on your journey, you can see what you've already overcome and what's coming next. You can continually use the tools in this book to help you move from one stage to the next with more confidence.

One of my mentors introduced me to Prochaska and DiClemente's Stages of Change model, which I have found to be incredibly useful when helping my clients through change.

The model states that there are six stages of change, each requiring different actions to take you to your required end-state.

After the explanation of each stage, you will find two questions that will help you determine if you're currently experiencing that stage of change.

Stage 1 – Pre-contemplation.

In this stage, you are unlikely to be thinking about making any kind of changes to your career. However, there may be a small inkling that's beavering away in your subconscious that perhaps there's some form of change you'd like to make but it hasn't yet risen to the surface. You're pre-contemplating, perhaps unconsciously, that you may want to make changes to your career.

- Does your work fulfill your needs? If yes, what led you to read this book? If no, why not?

- What engages you at work? Have you ever been engaged at work? If yes, what were you working on at the time? What did that engagement feel like?

Stage 2 – Contemplation

As the name suggests, at this stage, you may be considering making changes, but those changes are not imminent. You likely want to collect more evidence first. You may want to evaluate all your options to help you understand how to engage yourself at work. Or you may have plans about the kind of changes you'd like to make before you act. Hopefully, this book has been able to help you gather more of the resources you need to make the decision to act or remain where you are.

- If you could change anything in your current situation to make changing your job or career easier, what would it be?

- If nothing was stopping you making the next move to changing your job or career or making your current job more fulfilling, what would you do?

Stage 3 – Preparation

If you're at the preparation stage, you likely have some plans and ideas about how you see changes playing out, and you may have tested some of these already. You may now be looking for reassurance that you're on the right path. This book may be helping you see even more potential options and opportunities for change.

- What would you like to know more of in relation to increasing your engagement at work or in your career? How can you discover that information?

- What would reassure and support you to feel ready for the changes you wish to make? How can you get that support?

Stage 4 – Action

In the action stage, you're ready and primed for new beginnings, and you may be well on your way to making the career changes you need to help you feel more engaged in your working life. For you, this book may have supported your decision to leave your old choices and career path behind. Perhaps you've decided to change roles or change your whole career! These changes can be tough, and, as I've shared with you, support from many angles is beneficial when facing any kind of change.

- What one action will you take in your near future to take you closer to your goal?

- Who and what can help you on your journey?

Stage 5 – Maintenance

At the maintenance stage, you're well into charting your new path. You've seen some positive outcomes from your new, engaged state, but perhaps you've faced some reactions that aren't quite what you expect. Here, you're likely looking for reinforcement that you've made the right decisions and you need support to prevent you from returning to a way of working that feels more comfortable, even though it doesn't engage or fulfill you. The brain likes the easy pathways. This book may then have been the catalyst toward helping reinforce the idea that you've made the right decision.

- Who and what can help you continue following your dreams and your new ways of working?

- Think carefully about what encouraged you to make changes in the first place. Write these points down and put them somewhere you look often. They will serve as a reminder to keep going!

Recognizing your thinking.

Once you have a clearer idea of the stage you're at on your road to loving your work, it can be useful to recognize how your internal voices are supporting or hindering your efforts to move forward to the next stage.

There are some common ways in which the voices in our heads can sabotage us into thinking that we are incapable of getting to where we want to go. These are some familiar phrases you might be used to hearing the little devil inside your head saying to you:

- "You're not good enough."

- "You don't deserve good things."

- "What makes you think you can do this?"

- "Remember how you failed last time?"

But you can shift these voices to be more positive and help you move forward on your journey to creating a career you love.

Here are some ways you can hush your negative internal voice or shift it to a more positive perspective:

- **Notice when your critic appears.** I find that my little devil pops up at times when I feel stressed, anxious, or worried. The timing of the negative phrases is what assures me that what I'm hearing is only my inner critic catching me when I feel most vulnerable and it's not what I or others really think of me. This can be enough for me to ignore the critic or at least look for an alternative perspective that is grounded in more concrete thinking.

  o The next time you feel stressed, anxious, or worried about something, take notice: is your internal critic trying to beat you while you're down? Can you suggest an alternative narrative that may help you reframe your thoughts?

- **Create a silly character out of the critic.** This can help make the critic seem like a juvenile, non-sensical being that could never speak any sense.

  o The next time you hear your inner voice screaming mean things at you, give that voice a silly avatar to reduce its impact.

Note: These tactics aren't always easy to do on your own. Having someone you regard as a coach or mentor can be useful to support you in reframing your thinking. If the inner critics are causing you significant emotional distress, it's a good idea to seek out a psychologist or psychiatrist, who will be expertly trained to help you manage such issues.

Making changes when you have little time.

Once you know what you'd like to do differently and what it will take to get there, you may think that you don't have the time to make changes. However, if you prioritize the little time you do have to work on something that will bring you long-term joy, you will be grateful.

When you get to the point where you feel like you 'hate work' and lose the nuances of what you like and dislike, the last thing you might want is to spend your small amount of free time thinking about work. Unfortunately, this is the time when you need to do the thinking and find the time to make changes.

When you are aware of the areas of work you hate (and the areas you don't hate), you can begin to shape your career differently. That could involve searching for a new job or re-shaping your current role.

Get rid of what you hate.

Everyone has different likes and dislikes – it's what makes us human and unique. Try speaking to people in your teams to see which bits of their jobs they don't like, then think strategically about how you can find ways for other people to do the stuff you don't enjoy rather than wondering, 'How can I get this done?' If you're just trying to get it done without letting some-one know the tasks you're doing are draining, too difficult, or that someone else in the team might have a better skillset to do those tasks, more of the same tasks will keep landing on your plate, particularly if you're good at them and efficient.

It makes sense to invest in ways to remove the tasks you dislike from your to-do list. Michelle, one of my interviewees, introduced me to the rhetoric automate, delegate, relegate:

- **Automate:** How could you automate what you're doing so that a computer or system does the work for you? If you're not sure, who could you ask to help you find a way to automate some of that work?

- **Delegate:** Who else can do the work? Who can you ask for help? How can you spread the load? Perhaps there is someone else in the company who enjoys the work you dislike or who is better at that work than you. Giving work away that you can't do or don't like doing doesn't mean someone else will feel the same about it as you; getting that work might be a positive career move for them.

- **Relegate:** Is this an essential task for the big picture of your role or the goals of your team, organization, or customers? If not, maybe it doesn't need doing at all. That might seem like an impossible notion if you've been doing a seemingly important task for a long time, but spending time understanding the true value of that task and where it fits into the equation of what needs to be achieved might illuminate the ways in which the task could change or be removed altogether.

When there are parts of your job that you dislike, it can be easy to just accept that that's the way things are. You are given a job description to do the work that needs doing and you are paid to get it done. It seems somehow improper to give some of that work away to others or try to reshape some of your job so that you don't have to do the bits you don't like.

As I said earlier, few people enjoy *all* the work they do, but if those negative sides to your job mount up to being more than the positive sides, then you need to consider making changes. You have more control than you realize, and the more you take control, the more likely people will respect your boundaries. Ask yourself the following questions:

- Are there things you would like to do that you aren't currently doing? Why not? Is it because you don't have the skillset or the time?

- If you remove the things from your job that you dislike by automating, delegating, or relegating, what else could you fit into your day that you do like?

- What can you focus on outside of work that can help you build a skillset to do more of what interests you?

Other ways you can find support for difficulties at work.

Sometimes, with all the will in the world, you'll find yourself in a toxic workplace and whatever changes you try to make may always fall flat.

In this situation, you will likely have two options.

Option one: Stay with your company and possibly escalate the problem.

Option two: Leave the company and look for a position that better aligns with your skillset, desires, and needs.

Many larger companies have Employee Assistance Programs (EAPs). This is an impartial service comprised of trained people you can speak to who can help you to figure out what's going wrong at work and where you can get help.

If your concerns can be managed within that workplace, the EAP officer will help you find the support you need internally to help with your issue. If the officer believes that you have a more serious problem, they will be trained to help you find the correct psychological or physical support.

If you know of someone who you feel has shown empathy for issues at work, whether related to your current issues or not, try reaching out to that person.

Sometimes, confiding in a co-worker can help you manage a problem. A problem shared is a problem halved, as they say. However, be careful about who you choose to speak to; make sure you trust that person.

Know that you're never alone. There is always help at hand; you only need to know where to look for it, have the courage to ask, and believe in yourself enough to take the actions that best serve *your* needs.

Final thoughts.

Building a career you love isn't easy. There's a different path for everyone, and it requires frequent compromise and often sacrifice. Despite the difficulties, people who love what they do feel more fulfilled, energized, inspired, and engaged and they gain strength and energy from their work instead of letting it deplete them.

Is it worth the sacrifice? That's up to you, because you're the agent of your career, and only you can make it the career you want it to be.

INSPIRATIONAL QUOTES
FROM INTERVIEWEES

Throughout the interviews I had with people who love what they do, many of them shared inspiring thoughts about how they see the world of work. I hope these quotes are as much of a source of inspiration for you as they were for me.

"If people weren't out there pushing actively, a lot of change would never happen in the world. We wouldn't have a lot of things we've got now. It can be uncomfortable, but I think you've got to accept that uncomfortableness is part and parcel of making a change." Maurice.

"In my mind, everybody has so much potential to give, so the question is, are you going to take the chance to give it?" Lia.

"I really liked the advice that my uncle gave me once: 'You might not always do what you love, but the important thing is to find something to love in what you do." Sophie.

"Get your strengths, make them into super strengths, and you will do work that you love doing. Then mitigate, delegate, or automate your weaknesses." Michelle.

"Nothing is forever, career-wise. I've got a podcast and another company called Inspiration North, and we talk to people who have found their passions and purpose in life. You wouldn't believe the number of barristers who don't like doing what they do and have set up their own companies teaching people how to find and use their voices or the number of people on very high and fast tracks who just don't love their work, so they've started their own business. There are so many people who have left and started something new and made it a success. You just don't have to stay. There's peace in getting out of bad situations." Michelle.

"There's people who make things happen, people who watch things happen, and people who wonder what happened. If you're in that final category, given our modern world, that's going to be a very dangerous place to be. You can't sit back and wait for other people." Maurice.

APPENDIX

About the research

I always felt there was something odd about how we tackle employee engagement in organizations. I knew it needed a more personal approach, but, because it can be expensive and timely for organizations to create the systems and processes that help motivate people to do their best work, at first, I wasn't sure how to tackle the issue. After years of feeling like people at the bottom of organizations didn't have a voice, I realized I needed to give them one. The best way I know how to do that is by showing people how others who love their work have built their careers.

Over the last two years, I've conducted in-depth interviews, many of which feature on the *Love to Work* podcast, about the factors that drive people to love their work. I then analyzed the data using grounded theory, a qualitative research method that often begins with a semi-structured interview. I analyzed the transcripts using a coding process, while continuing to interview others to collect more data. Once I had reached what is known as a 'saturation point', where I felt the interviews weren't giving me any further insight into the answers for my research questions, I collated my results into a theory that answered my questions.

Using the semi-structured interview process requires a series of prepared questions to ask your interviewee, but you are not tied to those questions. You can allow the conversation to take its own path, exploring interesting ideas as and when they arise. This means that every time you interview someone, you allow that interview to shape the questions you ask in the next interview to help you ultimately hone the major factors that answer your research questions.

Research questions

The research questions are the overarching topics I wanted to discuss about people who love what they do.

These questions then informed the more detailed questions I asked when I interviewed people who love their work.

1. *Which variables influence someone to love their work?*

2. *Which qualities or psychological traits does someone who is self-engaged in their work have?*

About the interviewees

- 17 interviews

- Ranging from 35 mins to 1hr 5 mins

- 6 males/11 females.

- All people who love to work.

- Found on LinkedIn/in my personal network.

- Some work in-house at companies, some are freelance, some are business owners.

Job roles of interviewees

- Independent Artist

- Product Designer

- Building Services Engineer and Business Owner

- Medical Sales Rep

- IT Manager

- Financial Audit Manager

- IT Consultant

- Founder & CEO

- Organizational Psychologist x 2

- Co-Founder & Director

- CEO, Executive Coach, OD Consultant.

- Full Stack Web Developer

- Marketer and Writer/Freelancer

- Doctor: General Practitioner

- Psychotherapist

- Global Chief Data and Analytics Officer

Interview lead in.

As you know, the purpose of today's interview is to help me understand the journey you took to feeling engaged and happy in your job or career. To do this, I'm going to ask you a series of questions about your working life. The goal is to have an informal discussion about what makes you love what you do for work. If at any time there's a question you'd prefer not to answer, just let me know and we can move on. I'm excited to get started, so let's dive in!

Interview questions.

1. What do you do for a living? How did you end up where you are? Where did it all begin? What was the journey like?

   a) Have you had another career before this one?

   b) What level of education do you have? Have you ever gone back to school?

   c) Have you had any mentors/guidance/managers who made an impact on your work life?

   d) What inspired you to find this job/career?

   e) Do you have the opportunity for flexible working? Is this important to you?

2. What were the pivotal points in your journey that helped you shape your engaging career?

3. You said that you enjoy your work. What is it about your work that gives you this enjoyment? Have you always felt this way?

   a) Is the enjoyment daily? When does it occur?

   b) Do you/would you work evenings and/or weekends? Why/why not?

   c) Do you have a social life at work? Have you had times during your career when a social life was/wasn't present?

d) Do you have career goals? If yes, who sets those goals? How do you feel about goal setting? Is it important or not important to you?

e) What role does the organization you work for play in making your work engaging and satisfying?

4. What drives you at work? Has it always been this way?

5. How do you handle conflict at work?

6. In what ways do you receive feedback for your work? How do you feel about feedback?

7. What inspires you?

8. What percentage of your job do you enjoy?

9. What opportunities do you have to help others in your work?

10. What parts of your job give you the opportunity to be creative?

11. What does a bad day look like for you? What do you do when you have a bad day?

12. Where do you see yourself in 1, 2, 5 years from now?

13. What advice would you give someone who is starting out at work?

14. What part does work play in your life?

15. What part does the financial aspect of work play in your life?

16. What have you not enjoyed at work/in your career? What was it about that experience that you enjoyed?

17. What impact does the environment in which you're working have on you?

18. What part do wider world issues play in your work? Environmental/social/political, etc.

19. Do you work remotely?

20. Do you have any issues working with your team members when working remotely?

21. How do you manage to keep up to date with training and developments in your field while also having children?

22. As a woman, have you had any issues in a male-dominated industry?

23. What challenges have you faced in creating a career that you love? How did you overcome those challenges?

24. What do you know now that you wish you'd known at the beginning of your journey to creating a career that you love?

Reflecting on the research process.

Someone challenged me recently to consider how the process of writing this book has influenced what I believe about creating careers you love.

I've wanted to write a book for at least 10 years. I've talked about it so many times, and, honestly, I think most people thought it would never happen. I'm not even sure *I* thought it would happen. But I knew I loved to write, and I knew from the endless reading I'd done about writing that, to be a writer, and especially to be an author, you just *have to* write. You must keep writing and practicing and putting your bum in the chair and doing the work. There is no other way.

I also knew I wanted to study for a PhD. That had been a dream of mine before the dream of being an author. I completed my MSc in 2011, and although there were times when I had off-days, I loved it, and I still love research. I love discovering things and understanding why the human mind works as it does. It fascinates me.

The process of writing this book has been the same as working on my MSc. I have had days when I felt sure I'd throw in the towel; days when I felt that finishing this thing was an impossible feat, but I was determined. Not just because of the outcome of helping more people find work they love, but because I enjoyed getting lost in the process. Not all parts of it were enjoyable; trawling through the research was less fun than I thought it would be. Although, trying to write a book and analyze complex data while you have a two-year-old and are pregnant isn't easy! Despite that, the process excited me. The feeling of creating something, finding out something new, digging deeper – it still excites me.

My experience supports everything I've learned about loving your work; it takes hard work to build a career you love, but the hard work doesn't drain you, achieving it is satisfying and fulfilling.

I always remember when I was a 23-year-old writing a cover letter for a job I wanted. It said, 'I love to know what makes people tick'. That has never left me, and I don't think it ever will.

I don't see this book as the end of this process, either. Quite the opposite, in fact; this is only the beginning, and I'm so happy I've started this journey.

ACKNOWLEDGEMENTS

The TPPA crew – you know who are! Especially Wendy, who, in the last coaching session we had on the TPPA program, said to me, "Just keep going. Love to Work has potential." You rock.

My husband, Terry, who is my harshest critic and biggest fan. Without his tough love, I would never have continually got my butt in the chair to write. I love you.

My Mum and Dad for the endless conversations while I poured my heart out about what I wanted to do and how I didn't have the time to do it! And for always pushing me to do what I love. I love you guys.

My sons for giving me the time to write and think (sometimes!). I hope this book allows you to have happy working lives. I love you both.

The many friends and colleagues in my life who have continually spurred me on and encouraged me not to give up.

Every one of my interviewees, I am so grateful for the time you took out of your day to talk to me about your work. Thank you for trusting me with your thoughts and ideas. I found each and every one of our conversations fascinating, and I learned something new from all of you. I hope I've done you all justice.

To all the coaches who have worked with me, and to my editor, Maddy, at Softwood Self-Publishing, for ensuring I sound good and credible and for keeping me on a strict schedule!

To my book cover designer, Claire Smith at Booksmith Design. It looks awesome.

REFERENCES

1. Alase, A. (2017). The Interpretative Phenomenological Analysis (IPA): A Guide to a Good Qualitative Research Approach. *International Journal of Education & Literacy Studies*, 5(2). Retrieved from https://files.eric.ed.gov/fulltext/EJ1149107.pdf

2. Bolles, R.N. (2018). *What Color is Your Parachute? A Practical Manual for Job-Hunters and Career- Changers.* Ten Speed Press.

3. Bridger, E. (2018). *Employee Engagement – A Practical Introduction.* Kogan Page.

4. Brown, B. (2013). *Daring Greatly: How the Courage to Be Vulnerable Transforms the Way We Live, Love, Parent, and Lead.* Center Point large print ed. Thorndike, Me.: Center Point Larger Print.

5. Buckingham, M., & Clifton, D.O. (2001). *Now, discover your strengths.* New York: Free Press.

6. Cope, A., Whittaker, A. (2012). *The Art of Being Brilliant: Transform Your Life by Doing What Works for You.* Capstone.

7. Csikszentmihalyi, M. (2002). Flow: *The* Classic Work on How to Achieve Happiness. London: Rider.

8. Dweck, C.S. (2017). *Mindset. Changing the Way You Think To Fulfil Your Potential.* Robinson.

9. Fox, C., Webster, B.D., & Casper, W.C. (2018). Spirituality, Psychological Capital, and Employee Performance: An Empirical Examination. *Journal of Managerial Issues,* 30(2), 194-213. Retried from https://search.ebscohost.com/login.aspx?direct=true&db=pbh&AN=130373167&site=ehost-live.

10. Gelles, D. (2015). *Mindful Work: How Meditation Is Changing Business from the Inside Out.* Boston: Houghton Mifflin Harcourt.

11. Goleman, D. (2006). *Social intelligence: The new science of human relationships.* New York: Bantam Books.

12. Graham, D. (2018). *Switchers: How Smart Professionals Change Careers and Achieve Success.* Amacom.

13. Groskop, V. (2018). *How to Own the Room. Women and the Art of Brilliant Speaking.* Bantam Press. Guo, L., Decoster, S., Babalola, M.T., De Schutter, L., Garba, O.A., Riisla, K. (2018). Authoritarian leadership and employee creativity: The moderating role of psychological capital and the mediating role of fear and defensive silence. *Journal of Business Research*, 92, 219–230. Retrieved from https://www.sciencedirect.com/science/article/abs/pii/S0148296318303539

14. Hallowell, Edward M. (1994). *Driven to distraction.* New York: Pantheon Books.

15. Harari, Y.N. (2015). *Sapiens.* Harper.

16. Harris, D. (2014). *How I Tamed the Voice in My Head, Reduced Stress Without Losing My Edge, and Found Self-Help That Actually Works–A True Story.* Day Street Books.

17. Huffington, A. (2015). *Thrive: The Third Metric to Redefining Success and Creating a Life of Well-Being, Wisdom, and Wonder.* Harmony.

18. Kamenetz, A. (2018). *The Art of Screen Time. How Your Family Can Balance Digital Media and Real Life.* Public Affairs.

19. Keegan, M. (2014). *The Opposite of Loneliness: Essays and Stories*. First Scribner hardcover edition. New York: Scribner.

20. Kessler, C. (2019). How CEOs Are Making Mental Health A Less Taboo Topic at Work. *Fortune*. http://fortune.com/2019/04/18/mental-health-less-taboo-at-work/

21. Khan, W.A. (1990). Psychological Conditions of Personal Engagement and Disengagement of Work. *Academy of Management Journal*, 33, 692–724. http://dx.doi.org/10.2307/256287

22. Linley, A., & Bateman, T. (2018). *The Strengths Profile Book: Finding What You Can Do + Love to Do and Why It Matters*. Capp Press.

23. Mckee, A. (2017). *How to Be Happy at Work: The Power of Purpose, Hope, and Friendship*. Harvard Business Review.

24. Michels, B., Stutz, P. (2012). *The Tools: Transform Your Problems into Courage, Confidence, and Creativity*. Spiegel & Grau.

25. Morgan, J. (2017). *The Employee Experience Advantage. How to Win the War for Talent by Giving Employees the Workspaces They Want, the Tools They Need, and a Culture They Can Celebrate*. Wiley.

26. Nadin, G. (2018). *A World of Good.* CreateSpace Independent Publishing Platform.

27. Neill, M. (2018). *Super Coach: 10 Secrets to Transform Anyone's Life.* Hayhouse Inc.

28. Penman, D. (2012). *Mindfulness: An Eight-Week Plan for Finding Peace in a Frantic World.* Rodale Books.

29. Poundstone, W. (2012). *Are You Smart Enough to Work at Google?* Little, Brown and Company.

30. Rubin, G. (2018). *The Happiness Project.* Harper Collins Publishers.

31. Schwartz, B. (2015). Why We Work. Simon & Schuster.

32. Urquhart, C. (2013). Grounded Theory for Qualitative Research. A Practical Guide. Sage.

33. Weiss, J.H. (2020). *Moving Forward in Mid-Career.* Skyhorse.

34. Weiss, L. (2018). *How We Work: Live Your Purpose, Reclaim Your Sanity, and Embrace the Daily Grind.* Harper Wave.

ABOUT THE AUTHOR

Rebecca Longman is an employee engagement strategist and founder of the Let's Love to Work initiative, a coaching agency and an employee engagement and motivation information repository for employees and business owners alike. With an MSc in Occupational Psychology, she has been applying psychology at work, both in-house and as an external consultant, in employee engagement solutions, design, and communications and has been writing about engagement and motivation for the last 13 years. She is a sought-after speaker and guest writer within the industry.

Her blog, podcast, and social media channels each have a strong and growing following and can be found @LetsLovetoWork.

You can find out more at: www.letslovetowork.com